Are

Third Day Christian?

RU3D

CREATION
HOUSE

Sammy Rodriguez

ARE YOU A THIRD DAY CHRISTIAN? by Sammy Rodriguez
Published by Creation House
A part of Strang Communications Company
600 Rinehart Road
Lake Mary, Florida 32746
www.creationhouse.com

Unless otherwise noted, all Scripture quotations are
from the New King James Version of the Bible.
Copyright © 1979, 1980, 1982 by Thomas Nelson,
Inc., publishers. Used by permission.

Scripture quotations marked KJV are from the King
James Version of the Bible.

Scripture quotations marked NCV are from The Holy
Bible, New Century Version. Copyright © 1987, 1988,
1991 by Word Publishing, Dallas, Texas 75039. Used
by permission.

Scripture quotations marked NIV are from the Holy
Bible, New International Version. Copyright © 1973,
1978, 1984, International Bible Society. Used by permission.

Scripture quotations marked THE MESSAGE are from
The Message, copyright © 1993, 1994, 1995. Used by
permission of NavPress Publishing Group.

Cover and interior design by Pat Theriault

Library of Congress Catalog Card Number: 00-105441
International Standard Book Number: 0-88419-730-1

0 1 2 3 4 5 6 7 VERSA 8 7 6 5 4 3 2 1
Printed in the United States of America

Gladys
Toro

I dedicate this book

to my grandfather, Randolph Nunez Abreu.

Your passion is now my purpose.

I will see you in the eternal Third Day!

CONTENTS

Revive
the
Third Day
Lions and
Lambs

There must be more, *there must be more*, **there must be more!** I was raised in a Pentecostal church; I saw the "bakes, the shakes and the quakes." Yet one resounding echo reverberated within the walls of my spirit—*there must be more.* This echo became the cry of my spirit, the shout of my soul and the desire of my heart.

Metamorphically, this echo reflected the anxiety of an entire generation at the crucial hour of the Christian church—a generation demanding one thing: More. **There must be more.** There must be more than religious fervor and denominationalism. There must be more than events, services, congresses, conventions, crusades . . . more than books, tapes and cassettes . . . more than television and radio . . . **more than fervor and fanaticism . . . more than movements and marches . . . more than strategies and manuals . . . more than geographical revival and a church here and there experiencing a new move, a fresh wave . . . there must be more.** There must be more than ministerial hierarchy, bureaucracy and organizations of men. There must be more.

MY YEARNING

This was my yearning at the end of the twentieth century.

Revival was spreading throughout different churches in geographical regions throughout the United States and Latin America. Yet a great desire and a great hunger prevailed. The entire body of Christ did not embrace the revival. The Spirit-filled, full-gospel church did not fully accept the revival. Why? Then it struck me.

> *After two days He will revive us: on the third day He will raise us up, that we may live in His sight.*—HOSEA 6:2

The Third Day church is a . . .

* revived,
* resurrected,
* living church!

> *But, beloved, do not forget this one thing, that with the Lord one day is as a thousand years, and a thousand years as one day.*—2 PETER 3:8

* **The first thousand years of Christianity was the first day.**

* **The second thousand years was the second day.**

* **On January 1, 2001, we begin the third day!**

In Scripture, the most powerful occurrences were realized on the third day:

* **Abraham offered Isaac.**—GENESIS 22:4
* **Hezekiah's years were added.**—2 KINGS 20:5
* **Jonah was kicked out of the whale.**—JONAH 1:17
* **Water was changed to wine.**—JOHN 2:1
* **Jesus was resurrected.**—JOHN 20:1

In the third day, the church will offer a sacrifice of praise.

Blessings will be added to the church. The world will not tolerate the glory and the holiness of God in His people, and it will have no other choice but to loose us from its hold as we awake out of the religious graves that have held us and prepare for our ascension into the presence of God.

Let us not ignore that, according to Hosea 6:2, revival is the first step. In the third day, God will not only revive us, but He will raise us up, and we will live in His sight. The question of the moment . . . **the question being heard throughout all the corners of the body of Christ . . . the question reverberating within our souls and within our spirits . . . the question in every preacher's pulpit, in every congregation in America and around the world . . . the question is: "Are we Third Day?"**

THE LAUNCH

Revival launches the believer into the third day. In the latter part of the twentieth century, the launching began. The entire twentieth century created the launch pad for this great shuttle called the Third Day church. The Pentecostal, Spirit-filled, Charismatic movements inundated and saturated the body of Christ. They are the largest, fastest-growing religious movements on the planet. But what we experienced earlier—even in the latter part of the 1990s—were the raindrops, the drizzle, of the greatest outpouring of God's glory, presence and anointing ever witnessed in the history of the church. Welcome to revival—not just raindrops or drizzle, but the full outpouring.

After two days He will revive us.—HOSEA 6:2

The first two thousand years of Christianity are, in all practicality, completed. Welcome to the third day. God has promised to revive us on this third day.

WHAT IS REVIVAL?

Revival, what a term—overphrased, overused, ill-defined, misunderstood, manipulated, misinterpreted, exploited and exaggerated. Some ask for it, yet once they receive it they reject it. Some cry for it, yet once they receive it they establish committees and resolutions to control it. Revival, what a term. But it goes beyond a term; it is God's heart being poured out upon His people. Waking us up; preparing us for the next level. Revival is the catalyst to the journey. Revival is the first step to more. It is a step that every church, every ministry, every believer—you, I and the entire body of Christ—must take. Revival is the first stage.

> *After two days He will revive us: on the*
> *third day He will raise us up that we may*
> *live in His sight.*—HOSEA 6:2

Revival is not the end, but the beginning. To be revived is to be awakened. During the first two days of Christianity, the church collectively was not completely awake. In the past one hundred years, the church began to be awakened by the Spirit of God. The great Charismatic, Pentecostal, Full-Gospel movements across America and the world were the beginnings of the winds of revival blowing across the horizon of the body of Christ. The church was waking up. Beyond the bureaucratic miry clay of religiosity and man-made creative structures, the Spirit of God began to move in this past twentieth century.

God will revive us to raise us up

4

God will always wake us up in order to get us up in order to lift us up!

I would rather be lost in His presence than be found in this world.

to live in His sight. The church of God is experiencing revival. The body of Christ is experiencing revival. The army is experiencing revival. The bride is experiencing revival. The great, complete awakening will be fulfilled now in the third day.

FROM A LAMB TO A LION

So I ask you—What is God reviving? Whom is God reviving? The day of the lamb has arrived. Abraham partook of the first Third Day experience, and from him we get our first glimpse of the Lamb:

> *Then on the third day Abraham lifted his eyes and saw the place afar off. . . . So Abraham took the wood of the burnt offering and laid it on Isaac his son; and he took the fire in his hand, and a knife, and the two of them went together. But Isaac spoke to Abraham his father and said . . . "Look, the fire and the wood, but where is the lamb for a burnt offering?"*
> —GENESIS 22:4, 6–7

Isaac's question was answered two thousand years later when John the Baptist cried out:

—Jesus

> *Behold! The Lamb of God who takes away the sin of the world!*—JOHN 1:29

In the third day, God is reviving the lambs. Where is the lamb? Jesus is the Lamb of Glory. He is the firstborn amongst many brethren. Therefore, you are a lamb. In the third day we discover in God's presence our true identity.

Who am I? And who are you?

5

* **The world would say, "Know yourself first, and then attempt to know God."**

* **But in the third day, in knowing God I know myself, and in finding God I find myself.**

Without God, I am nothing. Without God I am lost. Without God I exist not. Blaise Pascal declared, "I believe, therefore, I am." There is no identity outside of Jesus. Outside of God I cannot know myself. But in Jesus I find myself.

In Him I am:

* **More than a conqueror**—ROMANS 8:37
* **The salt of the earth**—MATTHEW 5:13
* **The light of the world**—MATTHEW 5:14
* **A reasonable service**—ROMANS 12:1
* **An iron pillar and a wall of bronze**
  —JEREMIAH 1:18

The moment God finds me and I find Him, my objective is to lose myself again—but this time in Him. *O God, let me be lost in Your presence. Permit me to lose my identity, my objectives and my dreams. Let me be lost at the cross, never to be found, but always secured in the shadow of Your wings.*

* **Christ was crucified a lamb,**
* **resurrected a lion and**
* **will return on a white horse.**

Jesus Christ is both a lamb and a lion. We are both lambs and lions. But during the first and second days, we had these identities mixed up.

* **In the first day we were lions on the inside and lambs on the outside.**
* **In the second day we were lambs on the inside and lambs on the outside.**

6

✳ **But in the third day, we are lambs on the inside and lions on the outside.**

The revival shout coming from heaven is nothing more than God telling His people, "Wake up! Wake up and defeat the serpent! Wake up and defeat the lions of the Roman coliseums!"

✳ **In the first day, the lions in the Roman coliseums prevailed.**

✳ **In the third day, the Lion of the tribe of Judah shall reign!**

O God, revive the Third Day lions. In the first day, we were devoured by the Roman lions; in the third day, we will reign with the Lion of the tribe of Judah. If Jesus is the Lion of the tribe of Judah, then we are co-lions in the world today. We are the lions of the Third Day church. Our lion duty asks more of us than just a controversial or questionable roar in the midst of a glorious service. It goes beyond a temporal superficial expression that can come from the vocal cords of an individual. I speak of the reigning authority of the Lion. I speak of the power and the anointing of Him who is the Lion of the tribe of Judah.

✳ **In the first day, we ran away from the arrows of the enemy.**

✳ **But in the third day, we will bend the bow of bronze.**

Therefore submit to God. Resist the devil and he will flee from you.—JAMES 4:7

We will bend the bow and make him run. What a remarkable scene. What a remarkable picture God paints us in the Eighteenth Psalm.

*In my distress I called to the LORD; I cried
to my God for help. From his temple he
heard my voice; my cry came before him,
into his ears. The earth trembled and
quaked, and the foundations of the mountains shook; they trembled because he was
angry. Smoke rose from his nostrils; consuming fire came from his mouth, burning coals blazed out of it. He parted the
heavens and came down; dark clouds were
under his feet.* —PSALM 18:6–9, NIV

God, in His zealousness and passion for you, will part
waters, mountains and seas just to get to you. There is
not one thing in creation that can stand in His way. Not
even the clouds are fast enough to evade Him as He
rushes to your aid. He rides on the wings of angels to
speed His arrival:

*He mounted the cherubim and flew; he
soared on the wings of the wind. He made
darkness his covering, his canopy around
him—the dark rain clouds of the sky.*
——PSALM 18:10–11, NIV

This is the priority God sets on helping you with your
problems and circumstances. He lifts them from your surroundings and lays the burden on His back. Hallelujah!

*Out of the brightness of his presence clouds
advanced, with hailstones and bolts of lightning. The LORD thundered from heaven; the
voice of the Most High resounded. He shot
his arrows and scattered the enemies, great
bolts of lightning and routed them. . . . He*

brought me out into a spacious place; he rescued me because he delighted in me . . . .He trains my hands for battle; my arms can bend a bow of bronze.—PSALM 18:12–14, 19, 34, NIV

Why does God train my hands for battle? Because He has empowered me to defeat the enemy. Why bend the bronze bow? Because it is not gold—it is bronze. Bronze is an imitation of gold. It may look like gold, but it is not gold. Satan imitates God, but he is not God. God equips you with the power to snatch away the very weapons of Satan in order to alter his attack. Instead of afflicting you with his arrows, he is afflicted by his own arrows, which return back to him. As his own weapons turn to attack him, he begins to flee.

He makes my storm His canopy so His light can shine on me.

Bend the bow! In the second day we spent most of our time dodging his arrows. In the third day we have the anointing to bend the bow.

The LORD will cause your enemies who rise against you to be defeated before your face; they shall come out against you one way and flee before you seven ways.—DEUTERONOMY 28:7

Let God arise, let His enemies be scattered; let those also who hate Him flee before Him.—PSALM 68:1

9

Make him run, make him run, make him run away. The anointing and glory should be so strong upon your life that the enemy will run away. The anointing of the tribe of Judah should be so strong upon your life that the serpent will slither away.

✳ **In the first day we feared the devil.**

✳ **But in the third day the devil will fear us.**

He has put a new song in my mouth— praise to our God; many will see it and fear, and will trust in the LORD.
—PSALM 40:3

In the third day, praise will return to its scriptural purpose. There exists a praise within the depth of our being that will provoke the enemy to fear us. The psalmist was saying that from the depth of his being he searched and found a praise—and at its release, Hades closed its gates. What a powerful revelation. God does not shut down hell when we praise. It is the enemy himself that shuts the gates.

Why should we deal with the effects of sin every Sunday morning when we can address the causes of sin?

The praise of a saint is more torturous to the enemy than the fire of hell. We praise to get Satan out of the way, the flesh out of the way, the world out of the way. We worship to bring God in. Praise gets the devil out. Worship gets God in. We must roar until all the serpents have fled. Great Third Day services and meetings will occur when the saints begin as lions and end as lambs.

10

FOUR REASONS THE DEVIL CANNOT TOUCH US

The devil cannot kill us. The devil cannot even touch us. In the third day the devil will fear us; we will not fear him. There are four reasons why we will no longer fear him.

1 *We are hidden in Christ Jesus.* Every time the devil

looks for me, he ends up finding Jesus. When he sends demons to look for you, the demons will return empty-handed and tell him, "We went to the address you gave us, and guess who was there? The same One who defeated you two thousand years ago on the cross of Calvary." That's because we are hidden in Christ Jesus.

For you died, and your life is hidden with Christ.—COLOSSIANS 3:3

2 *The anointed ones cannot be touched.* As long as we are anointed, we are untouchable.

<u>*Do not touch My anointed ones*</u>.—PSALM 105:15

3 *We are already dead.* How can the devil kill someone who is already dead? If you are already dead, he cannot kill you.

I have been crucified with Christ; it is no longer I who live, but Christ lives in me; and the life which I now live in the flesh I live by faith in the Son of God, who loved me and gave Himself for me.—GALATIANS 2:20

4 *You carry the marks of Jesus, and nothing bothers you.* The stamp of ownership is evident upon your life. No one "messes" with someone wearing the colors of Christ.

From now on let no one trouble me, for I bear in my body the marks of the Lord Jesus.—GALATIANS 6:17

In the second day, we had it all wrong. We fought each other and sold out to the enemy in the second day.

* **In the second day, we were divided by denominational bickering; in the third day, we will be united by Spirit-filled revival.**

* **In the second day, we sat down in comfortable pews and listened to sermons; in the third day, we will stand up in the middle of our cities and proclaim deliverance.**

* **In the second day, we were victims; in the third day, we will be victors.**

Coming to the altar every day to repent for sins becomes a negative cycle of perpetual serendipity. We struggle continuously with sin that was forgiven two thousand years ago. The altar becomes more of a psychotherapeutic pillow than a spiritual place for renewal. We need to go beyond "I am a sinner saved by grace."

> The devil would rather hide in hell than hear your praise.

There must be a balance between both, and there exists such a balance. The Third Day people are well balanced, differentiating and distinguishing that before God's holy throne we are dual individuals. There is a dualistic identity to our being. We are

* **sinners saved by grace,**
* **and saints empowered by His Spirit.**

12

Our humanity is filled with His divinity. The apostle Peter, inspired by the Holy Spirit, established this fact.

By which have been given to us exceedingly great and precious promises, that through these you may be partakers of the divine nature.—2 PETER 1:4

✳ In the second day we simply survived. In the
third day we will succeed.

✳ In the second day it was the survival of the
fittest. In the third day it is the success of
the redeemed.

When will the children of the Lion of the tribe of Judah
roar louder than the lions of the Roman coliseums? I do
not refer to a controversial or literal roar in the midst of a
church service. **I refer to the roar of holiness . . .
the roar of passion . . . the roar of zeal for God's
truth and God's Word. I refer to the roar of a voice
crying out in the wilderness. I refer to the roar of an
entire generation in the midst of a troubled and per-
verse world. I refer to the roar of legitimate
praise and worship.** When will the cubs of the Lion
of the tribe of Judah make more noise than the lions of
the Roman coliseum? When, Lord, when? For if He is the
Lion of the tribe of Judah, and we are His children, then
we are the lions of this world today. Yes, it is possible to be
a lion and a lamb.

✳ **We are lambs before God,**
✳ **and lions before the world.**

It is of the utmost significance to differentiate. At times
we have, in the first and second day, confused the robes
and the garments that we wear in
corresponding places. We are one
thing before the enemy and another
thing before God. We need to
approach all things with the respec-
tive attire.

We need to
become saints
empowered by
His Spirit for
His glory.

I will approach the enemy as a saint
empowered by God's glory, while I approach the throne

13

of God as a sinner saved by grace. I will approach the enemy and the world with my head lifted high and with a shout in my mouth, but I will approach the throne of grace prostrated on the floor with tears in my eyes and the silence of the <u>lamb</u>. I will approach the enemy fully armed as Paul exhorts us.

> *Finally, my brethren, be strong in the Lord and in the power of His might. Put on the whole armor of God, that you may be able to stand against the wiles of the devil.*
> —EPHESIANS 6:10–11

✳ **We must come before the enemy fully armed and fully clothed, but approach God naked and completely transparent.**

✳ **We are lions before the enemy, but lambs before our God.**

✳ **We are lions before the coliseums of the world, but we are lambs before the altar of grace.**

It is before the altar of grace that the true power of the third day emerges. There I understand that the lion obtains his authority from the blood of the <u>Lamb</u>. It is at the cross that the lions are revived. It was the second day church that returned to a legalistic mind-set, focusing more on the way people looked, dressed, smelled and tasted than on the reality of our righteousness in Christ Jesus. In reality, we replaced God's grace with a grace guided by law. Why? Do we not yet understand that God's grace is greater than the Law?

✳ **<u>God wrote the Law with one finger,</u>**
✳ **<u>but He wrote grace with two hands</u>.**

Are not two hands greater than one finger? It is important for the Third Day church to know that on the cross the Third Day lions are revived. We are reviving lions. To revive lions is to revive a roar and to revive kingship—rulership. We should be reigning, and we should be roaring. With our roars we should be letting it be heard that God is alive and well. It is through the blood of the Lamb that the lion obtains his power. The blood of the <u>Lamb</u> speaks louder than the blood of Abel.

> I will approach the enemy as a lion, but I will approach God's holy throne as a lamb.

> *. . . to Jesus the Mediator of the new covenant, and to the blood of sprinkling that speaks better things than that of Abel.*—HEBREWS 12:24

✳ It is the blood of Abel that said, "I am innocent, and yet I die."

✳ It is the blood of the <u>Lamb</u> upon us that says, "We are guilty, and yet we live."

The blood of the Lamb speaks louder than the blood of Abel. It is the blood that covers multitudes of sins. It is the Passover blood of the <u>Lamb</u>. His blood is more powerful than the Internet.

15

✳ The Internet connects me from here to Japan in 3.5 seconds, but the blood of Jesus connects me from here to heaven in a twinkling of an eye.

✳ Jesus went to the cross so we could cross to eternity.

* He tasted vinegar so we could taste new wine.

* He said it was finished so that we could get started.

Are there any lions in the house? Second day lions only roared; Third Day lions will do more than roar—they will reign. The reigning anointing best characterizes the power of the lion. Christ did a lot more than just roar out of the tomb; He reigned over His church. He reigned over the world, and He reigns today. Jesus Christ is Lord. The Lion of the tribe of Judah reigns and shall reign in fullness. Lions in the third day need to go beyond just roaring. They need to reign.

THE SILENCE OF THE LAMBS

As a Pentecostal in the third day . . . as a Spirit-filled person in the third day . . . what I have discovered is that the greatest expression that can come from a Spirit-filled believer is silence. The greatest shout is the silence of the spirit—going beyond verbal rhetoric and noise. What needs to be said? What can be said? When Christ looks at you, what can He say about you? All He sees is His blood, His mercy. As He looks at you, all He sees at the end of the road, if we are successful in the third day, is a little picture of Himself. No longer the appearance of a rejected sinner—but of a divine saint.

This is the question that arises: On the cross, was Jesus blinded by the sins of His people, or was Jesus blinded by His love for His people?

When He looks at you, He sees back to Genesis . . . back to Adam . . . and He sees in you everything He wanted in

16

Adam—and even more. You no longer look like Adam. Now you look like Jesus; therefore, your beauty is even more.

So here I am, finally. After breaking through the crowd surrounding Him, my greatest wish comes true—I am before His face. Amidst all the shouts . . . all the screams . . . all the dances . . . all the noise, I contemplate the words I want to say. What will I ask Him? What will I share with Him? What will I say?

His Third Day followers are men and women who have scars in their hands, vision in their eyes and love in their hearts.

I am now before Him. I see Him. And as I begin to open up my mouth, I discover one thing—in His pure presence there is nothing that can be said. What can be said when . . .

- ✳ **His scars say it all?**
- ✳ **His heart feels it all?**
- ✳ **His eyes see it all?**

When He lifts up His head, whom does God see? Not some dirty sinner begging for forgiveness, but a glimpse of Himself. Why Himself?

Like His, our hands have been scarred, our eyes have been tested, and our hearts have been broken. At the end of the road, when He looks at us, He sees perfect images of Himself—nothing less, nothing more.

17

At that moment, as I stand before His face, I discover that a silent lamb is much more powerful than a roaring lion.

Are you Third Day?

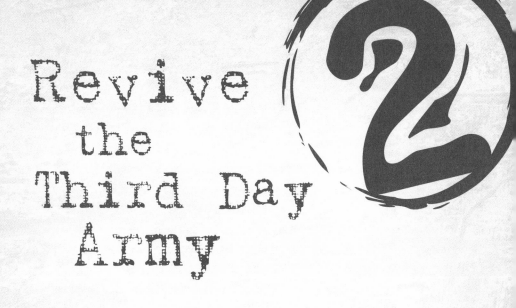

Revive the Third Day Army

No fear, *no fear*, **no fear**. Yet in the third day, there must be fear. Not the fear of the unknown . . . not the fear of the enemy . . . not even the fear of the great wrath of God . . . there must be the fear of the great grace of God.

After receiving so much grace, I fear arriving at the end of the road and having nothing to show for it.

I serve God not because I fear going to hell, but because I fear going to heaven. For when He asks me, "Were you part of My audience, or were you part of My army?", what will I reply? You and I are part of a second day audience or a Third Day army.

> *And Joseph said unto them the third day,*
> *This do, and live; for I fear God.*
> —GENESIS 42:18, *KJV*

You and I will both live if we fear God. The fear of the Lord motivates me

* to strive harder,
* to push further,
* to disappear.

> What greater pain can I suffer, if truly I am one with Him, than to cause His hands to bleed again?

I fear His eyes—not eyes full of anger kindled against me, but I fear the eyes of my Host . . . my Captain. I fear provoking those eyes to tears rather than allowing His eyes to see a shadow of who He is. I fear coming before my Captain, the Lord of Hosts, and attempting to explain to Him why I did not follow His orders.

I fear self-justificational rhetoric, excuses and bellowing with the comfort of my humanity.

I fear His hands—not the hands that discipline me with a rod, but the hands that discipline me with His scars.

For all of us, at all times, are either nails or ointment upon His scarred hands. Each one of us is either

✳ **a second day audience or**
✳ **the Third Day army.**

It goes without question.

In the second day, many of us belonged to audiences. We were comfortable. The spirit of comfort hovered and reigned over the body of Christ. Comfort attaches itself to an audience—not to an army. It is clearly related to an audience. We were comfortable in the second day. Comfortable enough to go to our churches and to our cushioned pews to hear comfortable sermons, comfortable praise and worship and comfortable altar services. We were comfortable. We were audiences . . . spectators. One would sing, one would preach, and we would clap in our pews as if we were at a Broadway show or listening to an opera. Beloved, we are part of the body of Christ. We are an army. We are the army of Jesus Christ.

20

* **The uniform of the body of Christ is not the religious, archaic, ceremonial or ritualistic attire and garb we have been wearing.**

* **The uniform of the body of Christ is the attire of a soldier.**

Above all things, my God is the Lord of Hosts. He is not the God of the defeated. He is not the God of those who are in bondage and chains. **My God is the God of the armies. He is the Lord of Hosts.** We are the army of the greatest revival. **We belong to the army of the greatest awakening. We belong to the Third Day army.**

At the end of the second day, many were fixating obsessively on preaching, teaching and articulating our dogmas regarding the Great Tribulation. I remember the great desperation, cynicism and anxiety that permeated the body in the latter part of 1999. The Y2K scare literally frightened God out of us. Churches and preachers instructed their members to hoard supplies in their basements and to create food pantries and shelters for the great doomsday that was coming. *Nothing happened.*

* **We are not the army obsessed with the Great Tribulation; we are the army obsessed with the greatest revival.**

* **I am not waiting for the Great Tribulation; I am waiting for the Rapture of the church of Jesus Christ.**

* **I am not obsessed with 666; I have already been marked with John 3:16.**

* **I do not care about the mark of the beast; I am covered with the seal of the Lamb.**

21

WOUNDS, SCARS AND MEDALS

I belonged, admittedly so, to a second day audience. I belonged to the audience. I was a spokesperson for the second day audience, because I feared the army. I feared the wounds of men and women of God who fought in the mission fields and battlefields of our streets and cities and came back tarnished, alienated, destroyed and weary. I feared those wounds. I saw and heard the wounds of the 1980s as many of our great generals fell to the side. Some of them fell on their own swords. I feared joining the army for those reasons. But then, I discovered great truth.

> **Wounds are not a tribute to your failure, but rather a feature of your success.**

* **The wound was not a negative marking, but a blessing scar.**

* **The wounds in the Christian walk do not draw you away from God, but closer to Him.**

The Christ we serve is a wounded Christ. What differentiates our God from the cosmic smaller gods in the nations that do not believe in our God . . . what makes my God different from any other god . . . is that my God is the only wounded God. He is the great oxymoronic expression of a deity. He is the almighty, all-knowing, ever-present God who simultaneously is wounded and scarred. Wounds do not make you less perfect.

22

I speak to you who have been wounded throughout this incredible journey we call the Christian walk. I speak to you who have been scarred. Many have dared to ask God to remove the scars. But now, in this third day, I ask you why. Why remove the scars? Let every scar be a medal.

✳ Let every scar become a medal of His testimony.

✳ Let every scar become a medal on the uniform of grace.

✳ Let every wound, every battle, every tear shed . . . let every broken life . . . let every contrite spirit and shattered heart . . . express the simultaneous march.

March on, Christian soldier, march on. Press on, Christian soldier, press on. **Blow the trumpet in Zion; sound the alarm on the holy mountain. Let every one of my scars be a testimony of God's power. Let every one of my scars exemplify the fullness of His grace.** Let every one of my wounds be a shout unto all around me that will testify that I fought with God—and I won. Let them be Jacob's limp. Let me walk out with the limp as a testimony of obtaining the blessing.

Scars. I feared those scars. My fear of those scars provoked my fear of entering the army's ranks. Yet now I understand; now I am not bothered by scars.

> *From now on let no one trouble me, for I bear in my body the marks of the Lord Jesus.*—GALATIANS 6:17

23

I carry the marks of Christ. Arise, I tell you. Arise, I speak into your heart. I tell you, arise. There have been times, undoubtedly many, when so many tears were shed that the tears no longer flowed down the soaked cheeks of this wounded soldier. Rather, the tears dripped inside, forming in my heart another pool of Bethesda, a pool of stagnated water. There are times when I cried so loud that nothing

For every wound, for every tear, for every scar, we receive a medal, a promotion and a commission in His royalty.

came forth from my lips. My vocal cords refused to express any more pain.

All that came out was the silent shout, the silent cry of a broken heart and spirit. Now, in this third day, I know that it was for a purpose. All my wounds . . . all my scars served a purpose. They were my medals.

The Purple Heart is given to those who are wounded on the battlefield. Now I understand that in the third day we receive our spiritual Purple Hearts. In Scripture, purple does not reflect or define those who are wounded—it defines royalty.

THE ENEMY

* **Whom am I fighting if the enemy has been defeated?**

* **What am I conquering?**

I am fighting a defeated foe, one who was defeated two thousand years ago. Then what is my purpose in fighting? To make him aware that he was defeated two thousand years ago. To release the hostages that were taken captive by this defeated leader of the army of darkness. We won a war two thousand years ago. And for two thousand years the

The enemy was defeated two thousand years ago at Calvary's cross with two pieces of wood and three nails.

church has been taking back what was stolen. We fight not to defeat the enemy.

The Bible says that He triumphed openly over them and exposed them publicly.

> *Having disarmed principalities and powers,*
> *He made a public spectacle of them,*
> *triumphing over them in it.*—COLOSSIANS 2:15

Whom do we fight? Yes, we fight a defeated foe to execute the vengeance of the Lord. But more importantly, the greatest fight . . . the greatest struggle . . . lies within the walls of my own heart.

That is where the battle begins. That is where the confrontation really lies.

Sure, our battlefields are in the heavenlies, for we fight against the principalities and powers of darkness of this world.

> *For we do not wrestle against flesh and*
> *blood, but against principalities, against*
> *powers, against the rulers of the darkness of*
> *this age, against spiritual hosts of wickedness*
> *in the heavenly places.*—EPHESIANS 6:12

Sure, we fight in the heavenlies. But we also fight in the pews. We fight in the pews against the spirit of religiosity, against a second day spirit that reigns strongly over many congregations and believers. We fight against the spirit that dictates to us the order of God. We fight against the spirit that limits God, that censors God.

✳ **Who are we to tell God what He can and cannot do?**

✳ **Who are we to say that things must be in order?**

25

Sure, God is a God of order, but whose order? God's order. What we may interpret as chaos, God may interpret as perfect order. Even in the chaotic rumblings and twirls of white-water rivers coursing through the mountains of Washington and Oregon, there is a perfect symphony of molecules and cells that come from the river's rapid waters.

> The Third Day army is an army that believes in God being uncensored.

* **What we may see as chaos, God may call order.**

* **What God calls chaos, we may call order.**

The God of divine order spat on the ground and healed a man through that methodology. It is possible that our services and meetings—our lives—have become so structured that we have created another box, another ark of the covenant. Within that man-made box we have placed the gifts of the Spirit, the fruit of the Spirit, the anointing of God and God's precious Word. I argue that second day religion is the ark of the covenant duplicated. Just as God placed the manna, the ten commandments and the rod within the ark of the covenant, our hierarchical structures and man-made dogmatic beliefs have put God in the box. As a Third Day army, we must get God out of the box.

> Four Levites were necessary to carry the ark of the covenant, but it takes only one sinner saved by grace to carry the cross of Christ.

26

I refuse to put God back inside the box. Let Jesus live. We

have been wrong. We have the image of God sitting on the throne with a long, white beard and a rod and staff in His hand. In reality, the God I serve is the God of the Bible—the God of Zephaniah and Habakkuk:

The God of the Third Day army is the God who rejoices, the God who dances and the God who sings.

The LORD your God in your midst, the Mighty One, will save; He will rejoice over you with gladness, He will quiet you with His love, He will rejoice over you with singing.—ZEPHANIAH 3:17

Though the fig tree may not blossom, nor fruit be on the vines; though the labor of the olive may fail, and the fields yield no food; though the flock may be cut off from the fold, and there be no herd in the stalls—yet I will rejoice in the LORD, I will joy in the God of my salvation.—HABAKKUK 3:17–18

My God is a living God. He is not a religious, backward, introverted God. He is the God who dances over His people. He is the God who lives within His people.

* Let Jesus live in our pulpits.

* Let Jesus live in our hearts.

* Let Jesus live in our prayer lives.

* Let Jesus live in our holiness.

* Let Jesus live in our hunger for the Word.

27

✴ **Let Jesus live in our praise.**

✴ **Let Jesus live in our worship.**

✴ **Let Jesus live in our services, in our meetings and in our gatherings.**

MAKE THE MEN SIT DOWN

Let Jesus live. **Let sin die. Let the flesh die. Let all worldliness die. Let Jesus live.** The Third Day army is the army of the living Christ, not the dead Christ . . . not the religious Christ, but the living Christ. Our problem is that we have responded as though we were an army led by men.

The Third Day army is not an army led by men. It is an army led by the Lord of Hosts, the Captain of all armies—Jesus Christ, Lord of all.

It is time to make the men sit down.

It was nearly time for the Feast of Passover, kept annually by the Jews. When Jesus looked out and saw that a large crowd had arrived, he said to Philip, "Where can we buy bread to feed these people?" He said this to stretch Philip's faith. He already knew what he was going to do.

Philip answered, "Two hundred silver pieces wouldn't be enough to buy bread for each person to get a piece."

One of the disciples—it was Andrew, brother to Simon Peter—said, "There's a little boy here who has five barley loaves and two fish. But that's a drop in the bucket for a crowd like this."

Jesus said, "Make the [men] sit down." There was a nice carpet of green grass in this place. They saw down, about five thousand of them. Then Jesus took the bread and, having given thanks, gave it to those who were seated. He did the same with the fish. All ate as much as they wanted.

When the people had eaten their fill, he said to his disciples, "Gather the leftovers so nothing is wasted." They went to work and filled twelve large baskets with leftovers from the five barley loaves.

—JOHN 6:4–13, THE MESSAGE

It is important to note that on this occasion, a young lad gave Jesus the fishes and loaves of bread that Jesus multiplied to feed five thousand.

If the lad had not been a young person, he may never have given his lunch to God. We are all young in spirit. God is reviving in us a young spirit, a spirit of youthfulness.

> *Even the youths shall faint and be weary, and the young men shall utterly fall, but those who wait on the LORD shall renew their strength; they shall mount up with wings like eagles, they shall run and not be weary, they shall walk and not faint.*—ISAIAH 40:30–31

God is putting eagles' wings on you, my friend. **This is your time to fly. Regardless of your age, regardless of your time in ministry, this is your time to fly. God is shaking the dust from your wings and empowering you to fly.**

> *The word of the LORD came to me, saying, "Before I formed you in the womb I knew you; Before you were born I sanctified you; I ordained you a prophet to the nations." Then said I: "Ah, Lord GOD! Behold, I cannot speak, for I am a youth." But the LORD said to me: "Do not say, 'I am a youth,' for you shall go to all to whom I send you, and whatever I command you,*

29

you shall speak. Do not be afraid of their faces, for I am with you to deliver you," says the LORD.—*JEREMIAH 1:4–8*

We are an army of freedom. We need to stand up and shout out that which was shouted out in John 6:10:

✳ **Make the men sit down.**

While men are standing, God cannot stand. We need to tell men to sit down.

✳ **Sit down, flesh.**

✳ **Sit down, pride.**

✳ **Sit down, man-made dogmas.**

✳ **Sit down, spirit of bickering, strife and contention.**

God needs to be standing in order for the men to arise. This army with the fishes and the bread in their hands must make the men sit down.

We are called to root out . . .

Then the LORD put forth His hand and touched my mouth, and the LORD said to me: "Behold, I have put My words in your mouth. See, I have this day set you over the nations and over the kingdoms, to root out and to pull down, to destroy and to throw down, to build and to plant."—JEREMIAH 1:9–10

30

✳ **to root out sin,**
✳ **to root out religiosity,**
✳ **to root out the second day spirit**

. . . in order to pull down the strongholds.

> *For the weapons of our warfare are not carnal but mighty in God for pulling down strongholds, casting down arguments and every high thing that exalts itself against the knowledge of God, bringing every thought into captivity to the obedience of Christ, and being ready to punish all disobedience when your obedience is fulfilled.* —2 CORINTHIANS 10:4-6

Then, when the strongholds have been destroyed and thrown down, we can build and plant.

> *Therefore prepare yourself and arise, and speak to them all that I command you. Do not be dismayed before their faces, lest I dismay you before them.* —JEREMIAH 1:17

Prepare and arise. **Get up and arise. Get up and praise. Get up and run. Get up and live.** Get up and tell the devil to be quiet. Do not be dismayed before their faces, lest God dismay you before them. Do you know what this means, beloved?

Either we execute the anointing and defeat the enemy, or the Lord of Hosts will humiliate us before our enemy's face.

> ✽ **Beloved, you have no other choice but to join the army of God.**

> ✽ **Beloved, you must join the Third Day army.**

> ✽ **Beloved, you must execute the vengeance of the Lord.**

31

Otherwise, the Lord will execute His vengeance upon you before your enemy.

THIRD DAY WEAPONS

What has God placed in our hands? What do we have in our hands? Let me tell you what we have in our hands. We have fishes and bread. We have the sword of the third day, beloved.

* **Abraham had Isaac,**
* **Moses had a rod,**
* **Gideon had a pitcher,**
* **David had a rock,**
* **but we have fishes and bread.**

Fishes and bread

Indeed, we *are* the fishes and bread in the hands of God. Let us look at what God does with bread.

And as they were eating, Jesus took bread, blessed and broke it, and gave it to them and said, "Take, eat; this is My body."
—Mark 14:22

* **He took the bread.**
* **He blessed the bread.**
* **He broke the bread.**
* **He gave out the bread.**

The reason God is blessing you, my friend, is not for you to experience some type of emotional jerk, twitch or spasm. It is not for you to brag about a blessing.

God always blesses you before He breaks you, before He gives you out. God takes you out of your misery. **God takes you out of darkness.** Then He blesses you. **Then He breaks you. And then He gives you away.** What a powerful revelation. This is what God did with bread at the last supper.

The reason God took you out of hell, out of your sin was to bless you. And the reason He is blessing you is to break you in order to give you away. God is blessing you; I know He is blessing you. But we need to understand that in the third day, blessings are not given to us—nor received by us—for some purpose for self-gratification.

The reason God is blessing you today is because He is about to break you tomorrow.

* **We are blessed in order to be broken.**
* **We are broken in order to be blessed.**

God is blessing you because He is about to break you. Do not fear that breaking, my friend. It is the breaking process that enables God to distribute us proportionally to reach many rather than few. That breaking—a testimony here, an experience here, a revelation here, a word here—is a multifaceted breaking. It is the many parts, the many aspects of our lives that can testify about the One God, the One Savior of our souls.

Fish represents life in water. Bread represents life on land. We have life—even in the midst of the storm. And we have life—even in the midst of the desert.

I'm taken, blessed, broken and given out!

What do you have in your hands, my friend? You have a promise in your hands. Open up your hands now, because in your hands there is a promise.

Where the devil is, there is fear, bondage, despair, anxiety and confusion. But where the spirit of the Lord is, there is liberty.

Now the Lord is the Spirit; and where the Spirit of the Lord is, there is liberty.

—*2 Corinthians 3:17*

33

The sword

What else do we have in our hands? With what does the army of the third day fight? **We fight with the sword.** **Not only do we have fishes and bread, but this army has a sword. The sword of the Spirit is the sword of the Third Day army. The sword is the Word of almighty God.**

If God could make a king out of David and a warrior out of Gideon, then He can make a king and a warrior out of you.

The Third Day sword is the same sword, in power and anointing, as the sword of the Garden of Eden.

> *So He drove out the man; and He placed cherubim at the east of the garden of Eden, and a flaming sword which turned every way, to guard the way to the tree of life.*
> —GENESIS 3:24

The sword of Genesis 3:24 had three characteristics:

* ✳ **It was upright.**
* ✳ **It was on fire.**
* ✳ **It was spinning.**

1 *The sword was upright.*

34

We are an upright army, just and righteous. We are an army of holiness.

> *Pursue . . . holiness, without which no one will see the Lord.*—HEBREWS 12:14

> *For I am the LORD your God. You shall therefore consecrate yourselves, and you*

shall be holy; for I am holy. Neither shall you defile yourselves with any creeping thing that creeps on the earth.—LEVITICUS 11:44

The Third Day army is a holy army; it is an upright army. We are swords in the hands of almighty God. We, this Third Day army, fight with a sword in our hands, and simultaneously, as the army of God we are the sword in God's hands.

God placed us on this planet to realize what He has done in the heavenlies.

This Third Day army is the sword in God's hands, and we utilize that anointing in our hands at this time.

As God's upright sword, we bear the characteristics of righteousness, integrity, holiness and accountability. God said, "Be holy, for I am holy." We fight with an upright sword. We are an upright sword. We are not on the ground. We are not lying still. We are an upright sword.

2 *The sword was on fire.*

The remainder of the flesh of the sacrifice on the third day must be burned with fire.—LEVITICUS 7:17

The Refiner's fire will enable us to be a pure sword. Not only that, but it is a sword on fire . . . ablaze. **The Third Day army is an army** of **fire . . . of God's holy fire . . . of the fire of the Holy Spirit.** It is very important to understand something, friend. The fire of the Holy Spirit has been misconstrued and misinterpreted in the second day. In many Spirit-filled, Charismatic, Pentecostal churches,

It is the flesh that will be burnt with fire in the third day.

we have heard that the fire of God makes us dance, shout and scream.

I believe the joy of the Lord makes you shout, scream, dance and holler—but the fire of God makes you weep. The fire of God is a purifying fire. The fire

The fire of God makes you lie prostrate at God's throne before it empowers you to dance.

of God is a fire that melts away sin, unrighteousness, iniquities, imperfections and stains. It is the fire of God that quenches those things in our lives impeding God's full glory from being seen. The fire of God is a fire that burns away those things that do not belong.

* **In the third day, the fire of God will not make us shout, scream, holler, dance, twitch and jerk.**

* **The fire of God will make us weep, break and lie prostrate before His presence.**

Then the joy will come in. Then the dance will arrive. Then the song of the Lord will be heard. We are that army. We are the army of the sword of the Garden of Eden. We are the army ablaze with the Holy Spirit.

3 *The sword was spinning.*

We are the army that spins. Why was the Genesis sword spinning? It was spinning to protect all entrances.

The Hebrew word for the verb *rejoices (samach)* usually finds expression in an external response—a spontaneous, unsustained feeling of jubilance, such as skipping about or spinning. It baffled me to understand from Zephaniah 3:17 that God, the almighty Creator of the universe, rejoices.

Beloved, God spins upon our praise. Every time we praise

and worship, God begins to spin and rejoice. That sword in the Garden of Eden was rejoicing. Rejoicing to spin around. Why do we rejoice? Why should we spin? In order to protect all entrances. Every time we rejoice, we are telling the enemy he cannot come in through the North, the South, the East or the West.

God rejoices over us.

God tells the enemy, "There is no entrance for you. Henceforth, I have liquidated . . . annihilated . . . shut down the entrances, for I am rejoicing at this hour over My people." I encourage you right at this moment, there in your room, in your office, wherever you may be, to rejoice.

* **Rejoicing is not the clapping of hands.**

* **Rejoicing is not a shout, a holler or a scream.**

* **Rejoicing is to spin as a tornado in God's glory.**

The spinning gesture represents continuous mobility. God's Third Day army must be mobile. All stagnant, dormant warriors are prohibited from God's army. The trench philosophy of twentieth-century armies has been replaced by God's agile, mobile warriors. We, the Third Day army, must be agile and mobile, continuously changing and moving. As God rejoices over us, we rejoice also. We rejoice to let the enemy know that there are no entrances, no passages for him in any aspect of our lives. Rejoice, and again I say, rejoice.

37

I understand why so many second day Christians have had so much trouble rejoicing. When the windmill is spinning, it produces electricity. When there is no wind, the windmill will not operate. When the wind of the Holy Spirit is not blowing, there is no rejoicing, there is no spinning, there is no continuous mobility. That is why there is no energy in many churches and congregations across the world. Without the fresh wind of God's Spirit, many churches in America are closing shop and dying.

Armies of the third day don't wait in the trenches; they rejoice. They are upright. They are on fire. We

We are the army of Jesus Christ ablaze with the Holy Spirit, founded upon His Word.

are the Third Day army. Therefore march on, Christian soldier, march on.

* **March on with the fear of the Lord.**

* **March on with the battle scars that are medals.**

* **March on with fishes and bread in your hands.**

* **March on with the sword of the Garden of Eden.**

* **March on with the trumpet of God.**

March on, march on, march on. We are more than just the army of Joel 3.

> *Proclaim this among the nations: "Prepare for war! Wake up the mighty men, let all the men of war draw near, let them come up."*—JOEL 3:9

We are the Third Day army of Exodus 19.

> *Then it came to pass on the third day, in the morning, that there were thunderings and lightnings, and a thick cloud on the mountain; and the sound of the trumpet*

38

was very loud, so that all the people who
were in the camp trembled.—Exodus 19:16

We are the army that blows the trumpet in Zion. We blow the trumpet that will provoke all to tremble, shake and believe in the Lord our God.

Many have had differentiating views of this army. Sure, we understand the prophetic application of what is to come regarding this army, but we are greater than the army of Joel 3. We are the army of John 3:16.

> *For God so loved the world that He gave*
> *His only begotten Son, that whoever*
> *believes in Him should not perish but*
> *have everlasting life.—John 3:16*

We are the army of the redeemed of the Lord. Let the redeemed of the Lord say so with divine violence.

> *The kingdom of heaven suffers violence,*
> *and the violent take it by force.—Matthew 11:12*

Now is the time.

> *To everything there is a season, a time for*
> *every purpose under heaven: A time to be*
> *born, and a time to die; a time to plant,*
> *and a time to pluck what is planted; . . . a*
> *time to love, and a time to hate; a time of*
> *war, and a time of peace.—Ecclesiastes 3:1–2, 8*

39

* For two thousand years, we have fought as a religion.

* For two thousand years, we have fought as an organization.

* **For two thousand years, we have fought as a denomination.**

* **For two thousand years, we have fought as a ministry.**

But I want the devil to know something. He can stop a denomination, a ministry and an organization, but he cannot stop the army of Jesus Christ!

> "No weapon formed against you shall
> prosper, and every tongue which rises
> against you in judgment you shall condemn.
> This is the heritage of the servants of the
> LORD, and their righteousness is from Me,"
> says the LORD.—ISAIAH 54:17

We are not just an organization or a movement. We are the army of Jesus Christ!

> Upon this rock I will build my church; and
> the gates of hell shall not prevail against
> it.—MATTHEW 16:18, KJV

We are a loud army. We have been silent for too long. We were silent lions when we should have been roaring lions.

* **We were silent in the 1800s with Charles Darwin and Friedrich Nietzsche.**

* **We were silent in the 1930s with Sigmund Freud.**

* **We were silent in 1963 when prayer was taken out of our schools.**

* **We were silent in 1973 when abortion was legalized.**

But in the third day, we will not be silent!

> *Now the Lord spoke to Paul in the night by a vision, "Do not be afraid, but speak, and do not keep silent; for I am with you, and no one will attack you to hurt you; for I have many people in this city."*—Acts 18:9–10

* **The Third Day army's mandate is not about members in the church; it is about worshipers in the temple.**

* **The army's mandate is not about a membership card in your pocket; it is about the anointing upon your life.**

This is the army of Jesus freaks.

> *For the message of the cross is foolishness to those who are perishing, but to us who are being saved it is the power of God.*
> —1 Corinthians 1:18

We are an army that is going to baffle the enemy. We are the third generation of Jacob. We are the army. The Third Day army fights on its knees, fights *in* the Word and *through* the Word. The Third Day army is the army of the sword of the Garden of Eden—ablaze. It is an army that is upright, on fire and spinning around. Demonstrating continuous mobility, continuous conquering. We are the Third Day army. Army, arise in the schools, in the colleges and in the universities. **Arise, Third Day army!**

41

THE FINAL MISSION

How do we measure victory? What differentiates a victory from a defeat? What is the mission of the Third Day army? The mission begins:

Marching orders given, I read with the utmost anxiety the mission of my life. After all these years, finally my mission is revealed: "Reach the prison where the most important prisoners of war are being held. Rescue them, and return home safely." So I march as a warrior with the intent of honoring my Lord with unadulterated success.

I arrive at the gate of the city. Immediately I am saturated with the sounds of mortar shells, stray bullets and chaos. Screams and cries of desperation fill the air with the sharpness of a bayonet. Around me, many great warriors of the Third Day army lie fatally wounded. Spared from these fatal wounds, as if divine providence shielded me for this hour, I press on toward the mark.

With missiles flying, warriors dying, smoke filling my surroundings to such an extent that the only visible color was the red, crimson blood of a wounded Third Day warrior, I finally arrive at the door of what I believe to be the place. Exhausted and weary, I inquire of the wounded enemy soldier, "Where are the prisoners?" Without uttering one word, the soldier points toward a building. On the outside, the building resembled a miniature version of a palace. A palace with stains, bullet holes, cracks and rubble, yet nevertheless a palace. Finally, I arrive. Darkness, like a canopy, covered the staircase leading toward the corridor of life's imprisonment. I progressed ever so slowly as visibility came from faith and not by sight.

42

At last I arrive at the end of the corridor. I hear the grunts, moans and indiscernible verbiage coming from a cell. The entire palace is empty. On the bottom floor I discover a prison cell that holds an incoherent, possibly delusional, warrior with whom I must return. Documentation lies on the ground outside his cell. Without any mention of his name, it speaks about him.

His captors describe him as a great threat to the kingdom of darkness. His captors found it necessary to employ manipulation, pride, envy, jealousy, religion—even success—to control and finally bind this man. My obsession with this man became my primary focus. Who is this man who has provoked such fear in the kingdom of darkness?

Finally I open the door of his cell. As a child anticipating the arrival of a marvelous gift, I yell, "Come forth. You are free!" The man does not reply. Again I yell, "Come forth! You are free." The man does not reply. Suddenly, I feel frustration as I have never experienced before. "Do you know how far I've traveled . . . how many years I've fought?" I say to him in frustration. I even attempt to show him my wounds, but he refuses to show me his face. Prostrate on the ground, he remains motionless. A third time I plead, "Show me it was worth it. Show me that my pain, suffering and rejection were all worth it. I have overcome so much to reach you, finally to free you. I plead with you, let me see this man whom I have struggled to free."

As a wounded lion arising for one more battle, I begin to see the shadow of the face of the man for whom I fought. To my astonishment, I am facing myself! It is I whom I freed!

At that precise moment, I discover that my mission is not to defeat the devil; he already is defeated. My mission is not to defeat second day spirits or religious bondage. My mission is not to rid the world from misery and sin, or somehow, through a messianic overture, to redeem the world again. My mission is not to prepare the bride for His coming, though a valiant effort that would be. My mission is to free myself from me. All these years I believed I was fighting to save the world. In reality, my battle is—and always has been—within myself. Somewhere in the inner confines of my palace, there is a prison where I must be set free.

Yet, there is another cell. I ask my shadow, myself, "How did I survive so long?" He points to the other cell. I am stunned by what

43

I see. It is He—my Captain, the Lord of Hosts! "How could You, with the power and right to be free, join me in my prison?" I ask.

He replies, "How could I rejoice with you on the outskirts of your palace when a part of you is bound in the inner parts of a prison?"

Finally, I make my greatest discovery. In the second day, I believed that I would find God exclusively in the largest of churches, in the masses attending crusades, on television or in radio, on posters and videos. Yet, in the third day I know how to find God. If I ever want to find God, all I need to do is to find the nearest broken heart or contrite spirit. I need to find the one locked in prison, in an orphanage, in a hospital room, in the prayer closet, on a street corner, in a midnight office.

Wherever I find a tear falling, a cry arising, a void awaiting or a hope springing forth—there, I will find God!

Are you Third Day?

Revive the Third Day Wine

3

Pressure, *pressure*, **pressure.** At the end of the pressure, there is the undaunted, uninhibited, unlimited, continuous sound of the ultimate end of breaking. The Third Day breaking point. The third day reflects, exhibits and exercises nothing less than continuous breaking points. Not just an obsession of breaking, but of breaking through. As Third Day worshipers, we break through to get to Him. In reality, what are we breaking through? If Christ broke through the veil with His death on the cross and His Resurrection, what do we need to break through?

> God breaks through our flesh and our humanity to get to us, and we break through from the inside out to get to Him.

I believe that in the third day there exists a dualistic battle.

The point of confrontation exists in one place: the wine press. Without question, the wine press is where we meet each other. The wine press embodies the place where God and a Third Day worshiper meet continuously. It is there where the pressure is put on.

45

The apostle John tells us of a wedding that took place on the third day.

> *On the third day there was a wedding in Cana of Galilee.*—JOHN 2:1

The circumstances through which we pass are not necessarily the works of the enemy against us. More importantly, they are the works of God for us.

Beloved, there will be a wedding in the third day. There is a wedding feast in the third day. This is the time of celebration. This is the time of rejoicing.

We know the story—it was Christ's first miracle. He changed water into wine. Before we focus on the wine, let's take a look at the wine press. How do you make wine? Wine comes from the crushing of the grapes. That is what we are. We are the grapes in the vineyard. Grapes can never produce wine unless they are crushed.

It is in the wine press that God crushes us. There the feet of the Almighty press down upon the lives of His people. I am under the shadow of the Almighty.

✳ **I am not being trampled by the enemy's feet.**

✳ **I am being trampled by the feet of almighty God.**

46

The feet of the Almighty continually crush me. They continually crush my flesh . . . my shortcomings . . . my inhibitions . . . my complexes . . . my insecurities. The feet of the Lamb crush me in the wine press until wine comes out of me.

You are being crushed right now. The circumstances

around you, the pressure you are experiencing—at times to the point of utter annihilation and complete surrender—are Third Day steps to complete vindication. But it is the necessary crushing under the feet of the Master. It is the Bridegroom who is crushing the grapes that will produce wine for the Third Day feast. You and I are being crushed.

WINE

Those things you are going through right now . . . the circumstances that at times perplex you . . . are more the works of God than the works of the enemy. God Himself is making wine out of the grapes. Even Christ was crushed. The greatest wine came not from the Napa Valley, from the fields of France or from the vineyards of Italy. The greatest wine came from the cross of Calvary.

Wine was produced from the hill of Golgotha. Christ was crushed. He became sin when sin He knew not. Christ was crushed . . . crushed by His love for His people. Crushed, and the wine of grapes was produced. We drink today from that two-thousand-year-old wine. What are we drinking? We drink

* **vintage grace,**
* **vintage forgiveness,**
* **vintage faith.**

No one could ever duplicate the wine of Christ. We drink from the greatest wine—greater than that at Joel's bar. This wine is greater than a spontaneous movement within our body in a great revival service. This is the cross of Calvary. We were watered down. We were limited to water, but **now we will drink wine, the**

In the third day the objective will be, "What can I do to make God dance, sing and rejoice?"

47

wine of grace. The unexplainable wine. **A wine of such utter beauty, taste, aroma and fragrance, never again to be duplicated. We drink the wine of glory . . . the wine of grace.** All who drink shall never thirst again. But we do undoubtedly feel the pressure of the wine press. **Pressure, pressure, pressure.** In the third day, you will experience pressure.

* **Watered-down religion will be changed to wine-filled revival, relationship and raising up.**

* **Watered-down preaching will be converted to wine-filled exhortation, revelation and impartation.**

* **Watered-down praise and worship will convert into wine-filled prophetic songs—the song of the Lord and worship that will bring about a new song.**

I believe that in the second day we were fixated, even in the Pentecostal and Charismatic world, with praying, "God, make me dance. God, make me shout. God, make me scream. God, slay me. God, do this to me."

Let our lives provoke the heavens to dance. Let our lives, testimony, holiness and integrity . . . the truthfulness and sincerity of our hearts . . . the transparency of our spirit . . . provoke a feast in the heavenlies. Let the angels join us. Let this become the hour when the church reflects the image of what it should be—a celebratory, festive, joyous, jubilant bride waiting for the Bridegroom to return. For in the third day, there is a wedding.

JESUS, THE WINEMAKER

Why were the feet of Jesus anointed by Mary? They

were anointed to crush. To crush on the cross the sin of the world. We are similarly crushed by Him, the Winemaker.

It is important for us to understand the revelation of the wine of the third day. It is not what some have imagined. We cannot limit Christ, the Wine-maker, to some emotional

The Third Day wine will not make you drunk or incapacitated. The Third Day wine will capacitate you.

experience in a service. We cannot limit Christ, the Wine-maker, to a twitch, jerk, shout or dance in a service. These things may very well be wonderful and exhilarating. They may be positive expressions in this great time of revival. But these things cannot in any way, shape or form completely embody the message of the Third Day wine.

The Third Day wine is much more than an experience of being drunk in the Spirit. The Third Day wine produces much more than spiritual drunkenness.

It will not take you out of your senses—rather, it will bring you to your senses. It is this quality that differentiates the Third Day wine of God from the wine of the first and second day. The wine of God will sober you up to the reality of the cross, of the Resurrection and of the empty tomb.

There has been much discussion regarding the spiritual wine from Joel's bar. Being drunk with the wine of God has been, for many, a goal to attain. There is some valid-ity in an overwhelming joy that makes you act, at times, as if you were drunk. Maybe in the dance . . . maybe in the shout . . . maybe in the exuberance. But the wine of God is not a wine that incapacitates you.

49

※ It is the wine that brings you to a higher level.
※ It is the wine that sobers you up.
※ It is the wine that cleans you up.

The wine of the third day is the wine of the cross. It is the wine of the Resurrection. It is the Winemaker Himself. Jesus is the Winemaker. On the third day, Jesus converted

Christ is making wine out of our experiences.

water into wine. But before He did that, He ordered that the water pots be filled with water. **In the second day we filled our water pots with water.** We filled our experience with theology. We filled our services with order. **We filled our sermons with structure and outlines. We filled belief systems with dogmas. We filled water pots with water.** Much of the water was clear, pure and good, but some of it was irrelevant. Some of it was actually inappropriate and impure water. But in the third day, God will convert the water into wine.

GRAPES, RAISINS OR WINE

We are either first day grapes, second day raisins or Third Day wine. In the second day—our raisin period—we accomplished nothing. For too long we stuck around in our trench warfare, shriveled up, dried up, wrinkled and unsuccessful. We spoke of wine, but we never became wine.

* We wrote it down, but never executed it.
* We saw it, but never obtained it.
* We dreamed it, but never accomplished it.

50

Do not miss the Third Day anointing. Do not miss the hour. Do not become a raisin. In the Third Day body, you need to be a grape about to be crushed. **Let the crushing begin.** Let the Master Winemaker—the Bridegroom—crush the church. Let the Bridegroom crush every believer. Let the Bridegroom crush me. Let the Bridegroom crush you. **Crush the impurities, crush the useless things out. Crush even**

the anointing out of us. Crush the joy ... crush the zeal ... crush the faith. Crush us until faith, holiness and power come out.

Friend, let every circumstance that comes your way become an opportunity to produce wine. All the pressures, pains, sufferings, challenges ... all the perplexities, quandaries, the entire quagmire ... let them all become a field of grapes.

In the third day, you need to convert your circumstances into a wine press.

You, by stepping out, possessing and proclaiming, can convert every circumstance around you into a wine press. All that is surrounding you right now is a vineyard. You are in the midst of the vineyard. Christ is the vine. You are connected to the vine, and now you have the opportunity to crush and produce wine.

ADAM VS. JESUS

I challenge you, as the Bridegroom crushes us to produce the Third Day wine, to be continually crushed by Him.

We have been living like Adam when we should be living like Jesus.

May He continue to eliminate within us the things that do not belong, until all that comes out is pure, 100 percent beauty. Pure wine, pure Jesus. In the third day, this great crushing activity by the Winemaker is essential. What is He crushing in us? He is crushing Adam. He needs to crush Adam so Jesus can come out.

And as we have borne the image of the man of dust, we shall also bear the image of the heavenly Man.—1 Corinthians 15:49

We need to bring down the heavenly, the celestial image.

51

We have greater potential than Adam. We have a greater promise. In the third day, we are not Adam.

> ✳ **We are not from the tribe of Adam; we are from the tribe of Jesus.**
>
> ✳ **We were not born into the death of Adam; we were born into the life of Christ.**
>
> ✳ **We were not created in Genesis; we were created in John 3:16.**

God gave Eve to Adam so that he would not be alone. He gave us someone greater than Eve. He gave us the Holy Spirit—the Comforter and the Counselor—so that we would not be alone.

> *But the Counselor, the Holy Spirit, whom the Father will send in my name, will teach you all things and will remind you of everything I have said to you.—JOHN 14:26, NIV*

Adam was covered with the skin, but we are covered by the blood of the Lamb. Stop living like Adam. It is time for you to start living like Jesus. You are not made in the image of Adam. You are formed in the image of Jesus Christ. If God enabled Adam to name every animal in the Garden, God has anointed you to name every blessing in the kingdom. You are not a son of Adam; you are a by-product of Jesus.

> God clothed Adam with animal skin, but God has covered us with the blood of the Lamb.

52

WHO ARE THESE PEOPLE?

After the Fall, Adam did not have access to the Garden. But you and I have access to the throne room of God . . .

to the throne room of glory. I do not want just His garden. I want access to Him.

* **We have access to the throne room of God.**
* **We have access to the heart of God.**
* **We have access to the ears of God.**

This is why the angels are perplexed at times. The angels must be perplexed by us. There must be an incredible amount of astonishment in the heavenlies. The angels must be asking each other, "Who are these people? What power they have that with one whisper, they can make the heavens shake. We sing 'Holy, holy, holy' for eons and barely make Him twitch or blink an eye."

But when one redeemed worshiper lifts a hand or whispers a sound, He stands up from His throne and immediately executes the prayer of that saint.

* **With one shout, hell begins to tremble.**

* **With one lifted hand to God Almighty, every angel snaps to attention with swords drawn.**

Who are these people who provoke heaven and crush hell? What authority do they have? From where does that authority come? Friend, our authority comes from the Winemaker. We have been crushed.

We filled our water pots with water long enough. It is time for the process of change to begin. It is time for water to be changed into wine. We are the Third Day wine.

* **We will bring joy to the desolate and comfort to the brokenhearted.**

53

✳ We will declare the year of the favor of the Lord.

✳ We will free the captive and raise the dead.

✳ We will pronounce the good news.

The Spirit of the Lord is on me, because he has anointed me to preach good news to the poor. He has sent me to proclaim freedom for the prisoners and recovery of sight for the blind, to release the oppressed.—LUKE 4:18, NIV

We are the wine in the third day. I've been crushed because God wanted to spread me and to fill other lives with the testimony, the joy of my life. The Winemaker has crushed this grape in order to share me with all the world. Now I understand

In the third day, the Adam in us must be destroyed so that the Jesus in us can live in fullness.

the circumstances. Now I understand the joy. Now I understand the reasoning. Now I understand the purpose.

JARS OF PURIFICATION

The jars of purification become the holders of new wine. Not just any jars—they were the jars of purification used to store the waters. They became the vessels and the instruments that created the catalyst whereby God changed water into wine.

54

You and I are being purified in the third day in order for the water inside us to be changed into wine. **We are not just any jars.** We are the jars that have been molded by experience. We have been molded by situations and circumstances. **We are jars that have** been molded in the prayer closets and in the secret place, at the altars on our knees and faces, prostrate and slain, weeping and moaning and groaning in an indiscernible language that is understandable in the heavenlies. **We are the jars that have been molded and purified.** The purification process is continuous. It is not limited to a moment, revival, conference or crusade. The purification process continues.

We are the jars of purification that become the holders of new wine in the third day.

* **This is why we have been purified.**

* **This is why we had to go through a process.**

* **This is why we were not chosen when we thought we should have been chosen.**

* **This is why we were not given an opportunity when we thought that we were the best ones for the opportunity.**

There was a time given, a process allocated by God Himself, predestined to hold us back for the third day. Why the third day? Because God saves the best for last. *On the third day a wedding took place at Cana in Galilee. Jesus' mother was there, and Jesus and his disciples had also been invited to the wedding. When the wine was gone, Jesus' mother said to him,* 55 *"They have no more wine."*

"Dear woman, why do you involve me?" Jesus replied. "My time has not yet come."

His mother said to the servants, "Do whatever he tells you."

Nearby stood six stone water jars, the kind used by the Jews for ceremonial washing, each holding from twenty to thirty gallons. Jesus said to the servants, "Fill the jars with water"; so they filled them to the brim. Then he told them, "Now draw some out and take it to the master of the banquet."

They did so, and the master of the banquet tasted the water that had been turned into wine. He did not realize where it had come from, though the servants who had drawn the water knew. Then he called the bridegroom aside and said, "Everyone brings out the choice wine first and then the cheaper wine after the guests have had too much to drink; but you have saved the best till now."

—JOHN 2:1–10, NIV

My friend, my brother, my sister, we have been held back until this time. You and I have been held back until this very season. We were not released in the second day because we were predestined to be released in the third day.

It was on the third day that Jonah was vomited out of the whale. We are being released. We are being vomited out in this very moment into the fullness of God's anointing.

We were stored up in the belly of the whale for so long, waiting for a time like this. We have felt that we have been travailing . . . tarrying . . . waiting. Our time of waiting is over. We are being coughed up onto Nineveh. We are being coughed up by the whale of religion . . . mediocrity . . . and comfort. We are being coughed up even by the whale of waiting, travailing and tarrying. The time has come for the great release.

THE GREAT RELEASE

We are being released at this very moment in the third day. Across America, Latin America, Europe, Asia, India and Africa, many Third Day worshipers are being released simultaneously. This is why similar miracles and manifestations are occurring in different parts of the world, without media coverage or access to technology and the Internet.

In tribes and villages across the world, the same miracles are being demonstrated and executed. An anointing as we have never seen before is being poured out. Jesus Christ is being exalted. The greatest revival is occurring now as we speak.

It is a revival where Jesus Christ is being lifted up and He is drawing all men unto Himself.

God saves the best for last.

* He never gives the best in the beginning.
* He never gives the best in the middle.
* He saves the best for last.

Let's look at evidence of this from Scripture. The account of Creation establishes God's "best-for-last" design.

In the beginning God created the heavens and the earth. . . . And God said, "Let there be light." . . . And there was evening, and there was morning—the first day.

And God said, "Let there be an expanse between the waters to separate water from water." . . . And there was evening, and there was morning—the second day.

And God said, "Let the water under the sky be gathered to one place, and let dry ground appear. . . . Let the land produce vegetation: seed-bearing plants and trees on the land that bear fruit with seed in it, according to their various kinds." . . . And there was evening, and there was morning—the third day.

And God said, "Let there be lights in the expanse of the sky to separate the day from the night, and let them serve as signs to mark seasons and days and years, and let them be lights in the expanse of the sky to give light on the earth." . . . And there was evening, and there was morning—the fourth day.

And God said, "Let the water teem with living creatures, and

57

*let birds fly above the earth across the expanse of the sky." . . . And
there was evening, and there was morning—the fifth day.*

*And God said, "Let the land produce living creatures according
to their kinds: livestock, creatures that move along the ground, and
wild animals, each according to its kind. . . . Let us make man in
our image, in our likeness . . . ." God saw all that he had made,
and it was very good. And there was evening, and there was
morning—the sixth day.*

—GENESIS *1:1, 3, 5–6, 8–9, 11, 13–15,*

19–20, 23–24, 26, 31, NIV

What did God create last? He created humanity. He
saved the best for last. If you read the full text of Genesis
1, you see that after God created each
thing, the Word says, "God saw that
it was good." But only after He created man does the Bible say, "It was
very good" (v. 31). We are much better
than just good; we are very good. We
are great. We are excellent, because God saves the best
for last.

**The last
outpouring is
the greatest
outpouring.**

God spoke through the prophet Joel concerning the last
days.

> *And afterward, I will pour out my Spirit
> on all people. Your sons and daughters will
> prophesy, your old men will dream
> dreams, your young men will see visions.*
> —JOEL *2:28,* NIV

The last revival is the greatest revival. The last experience is the greatest experience. Right when you think it
is over . . .

✳ **it is that final step;**
✳ **it is that final inch;**
✳ **it is that final push.**

Do not give up. Keep on crushing the grapes. Keep on pressing on, because He saves the best for last.

A NEW GENERATION

God saves the best for last. This fact alone demonstrates why Satan has, on so many occasions, attempted through the curse of abortion to impede many Christians from being born. We are about to see the most anointed generation of believers in the history of the church. They do not conform to the parameters or labels placed on them by the common folk. These believers are radical. Our generation, our Christian generation, is a radical one. We do not look like our forefathers, we do not speak like our forefathers, but we must declare that we have the same passion of our forefathers.

✳ **We believe in the legacy our forefathers gave us.**

✳ **We build upon the efforts, footsteps and foundations created by our forefathers.**

✳ **We appreciate the efforts—and the lives— our forefathers gave for the suffering of the cross.**

We must not be ignorant or naïve to believe that we are creating a brand-new thing. We must not come in with an arrogant spirit, believing that our thing is exclusive to us and that we will annihilate all from the past. The Third Day generation appreciates the legacy from our forefathers. The harvest comes from vineyards that have existed from generation to generation. Being the third day

59

does not nullify earlier songs sung in our churches or earlier sermons preached on our altars.

We do not worship revival in the third day. Neither can we worship worship.

I fear many have misinterpreted the purpose, the vision and the objectives of a Third Day person. A Third Day believer . . . a Third Day

The third day exemplifies the fundamental truths that have solidified our faith for generations, and does so at a higher level . . . with more noise . . . with more power . . . with more clarity.

church . . . cannot be obsessed with revival. We cannot be obsessed with worship.

✶ **We must be obsessed with Jesus Christ.**

✶ **We must be obsessed with lifting Him up, and all men will be drawn unto Him.**

✶ **We must be obsessed with the cross of Calvary . . . with the empty tomb . . . with Pentecost . . . with the upper room.**

✶ **We must be obsessed with the Word of God and its validity, with the infallibility and the proclamation of the Word of God, guarding it from wolves that would attempt to distort it.**

✶ **We must preach a revival from the cross.**

60

Revival comes from the cross. Revival is the cross. Revival is Jesus. The glory of God is Jesus. The anointing is Jesus. It is the power of God unto salvation. Nothing less and nothing more. But in the third day, God saves the best for last.

You and I have been persecuted, and we have suffered. No doubt there have been many attempts on our lives, attempts of which we may not have been aware. Abortion was legalized in our generation. Crimes against children have escalated. Children are the primary targets of Satan in the third day. Why children? Because out of the mouths of babes shall spring forth praise.

> *From the lips of children and infants you have ordained praise because of your enemies, to silence the foe and the avenger.*
> —PSALM 8:2, NIV

> *But Jesus called the children to him and said, "Let the little children come to me, and do not hinder them, for the kingdom of God belongs to such as these."*—LUKE 18:16, NIV

Beloved, I believe that a generation of young people, a generation of children, will emerge in the third day to revolutionize the entire world for Jesus Christ.

The most radical believers are being born today in hospital rooms, or they are on elementary, junior high, high school and college campuses throughout the world.

These are the most radical anointed people on the planet. These are the most dangerous people on Planet Earth. They will turn this world downside up for Jesus Christ. There is an anointing upon this generation— because He saves the best for last.

61

✳ **You are not alive at this time by coincidence.**
✳ **You are not alive at this time by chance.**
✳ **You are alive because you are the best.**

You are alive because God saves the best for last. This is your time to rejoice, your time to praise, your time to celebrate, because He saves the best for last. Your church will be the best because He saves the best for last. Your ministry will be the best because He saves the best for last. The anointing upon your life will be the best because He saves the best for last. **The hour has come.** **No more watered-down Jesus. No more watered-down gospel. No more watered-down preaching. No more watered-down faith. No more watered-down anointing. No more watered-down worship. No more watered-down teachings. He saves the best for last.**

NEW WINESKINS FOR NEW WINE

In the Third Day, new-wine Christians will arise. In the Third Day, new-wine Christians will march. In the Third Day, new-wine Christians will exercise the calling of the glory of God in churches and in pulpits around the world.

* **In the third day, they will not hold back.**
* **In the third day, they will not be limited.**
* **In the third day, they will not be intimidated.**
* **In the third day, they will not be shut up.**

Why? Because He saves the best for last. New wineskin is coming. The outer structure . . . the logistics . . . will see a great paradigm shift occurring in the body of Christ.

The denominations and movements that will succeed in the third day are those that are agile enough to recognize the cultural, economic and spiritual dynamics of the Third Day church in the body of Christ. This is not the same as the body of Christ of one hundred years ago. The body of Christ in the third day is much different. The body of Christ in the second day exhibited demands,

We are not limited by committees and boards, but we are released into the fullness of ministry.

62

expectations and desires. The second day body used technology and exhibited fervor and zeal.

In this third day, each of these factors must still be considered in the board rooms and executive offices of ministries, organizations and denominations throughout the world. But only those who are agile . . . who are willing to change the wineskins before the water is converted into wine . . . will succeed and flourish.

Those who continue to preoccupy themselves with the old wineskin—rather than creating a new wineskin to hold the new wine—will perish. The third day is not about the wineskin. It is about the wine. Even more importantly, it is not about the wine; it is about the Winemaker.

THE THIRD DAY WEDDING

In the third day, there is a wedding. Are you ready for the wedding? We are part of the wedding party. We have all assembled. Rehearsals and practices are over, and now we wait. We await the appearance in this wedding. We await the music to be played in order for the party to march in. Waiting for the bride to meet the Bridegroom at the altar. We are waiting for the wedding song to be played. We await the wedding march that will cause all to arise. Then the bride will make her great entrance, dressed in a pearly white dress without wrinkles and stains. Here we are . . . **waiting, waiting, waiting.** In the third day, the song must be heard. It must be the wedding march song. Not just a uniform song or a marching song or an army song.

63

* In the third day, we will be wearing not only the uniforms of soldiers.

* In the third day, we will be dressed for the wedding party.

I am waiting to see if this time, as the Holy Spirit lifts up the veil, He will present this bride to the Bridegroom. Will the Spirit see the glory of God on the face of this bride? Perhaps the reason why He has not returned yet is because the Spirit is waiting until He sees the glory of God on the face of the bride. Maybe the glory is not there yet. At times, bickering, division and strife have scarred up the face of the bride.

> The Holy Spirit cannot present to the Bridegroom a church with anything less than the glory of God on her face.

In the third day, the church must exhibit the glory of God upon her face. When the veil is lifted, what will the Holy Spirit see? Let it be the glory of God. If the glory of God is seen on the face of the church, the church will finally be able to be presented to the Bridegroom, and the wedding ceremony will, after two thousand years, finally take place.

THE FINAL CRUSH

The crushing process is so torturous that it is difficult to describe. Crushing doesn't come from God's rod or staff hitting or punishing us. God tortures us differently. In the midst of my pain and desperation, I cried out and asked God why. "Why? Why?

64

* "Why do You insist on visiting me?

* "Why do You torture me with Your grace?

* "Why do You persecute me with Your forgiveness?

* "Why do You surround me with Your mercy?

* "Why do You punish me with Your love?

✳ **"Why do You continue to follow me even when I turn my back on You?"**

"Why?" I ask, "am I not crushed by Your wrath or Your anger or Your fire?" It is ironic that in the third day, He burns me, creates me and builds me with His fire and glory. Why, why, why the crush?

I begin by pleading with Him to stop, and I finish by begging Him to continue.

In the third day, more and more we will desire not to be lifted up by His hands to the highest of places, but to be crushed by the sole of His feet in the solemnest of places. "Let me be crushed in the valley any day rather than to be lifted up on the mountaintop without You."

Are you Third Day?

Revive Us With Third Day Principles

They wait, *they wait*, **they wait**—in full anticipation of the coming glory, the greatest revival of ultimate outpouring. They wait . . .

✳ **Nowhere, yet everywhere**
✳ **Hidden, yet truly visible**
✳ **In the shadows, yet in the spotlight**

They wait. Waiting, anticipating, yearning, desiring, hungering for the greatest, for the ultimate, for the best—for God, uncensored, uninhibited, unlimited and undeterred.

They search for God in His fullness. Not a God censored by man, religion, programs or ideas, but a God free to be God.

They wait. In prayer closets, at the altars, on their knees, in basements and in upper rooms, they wait. These folks, the strange ones, the fanatics, the freaks, the radicals, the ludicrous, the absurd and the foolish, they all wait.

Where are they? They are everywhere.

✳ **In the aisles and in the pews**

* At the altars and in the pulpits

* In the choir rooms and in the Sunday school classes

* On Wall Street and in the Silicon Valley

* On the farms of Nebraska and in the fields of Argentina

They are everywhere . . . in ghettos and in mansions, in suburbs and in cities. They are black. They are white. They are brown. They are yellow. They are red. And although there exist many languages and many faces, one spirit, one desire, one anointing, one calling is being released in the third day. In the third day, there are fools, freaks, radicals and fanatics. Each is different. Not satisfied with religion, they anticipate more of God, from God and in God. How foolish they must they be to believe that the Word is infallible. How naïve they must be to believe they can do all things through Christ who gives them strength.

How ludicrous the expectation that they shall actually do greater things in the name of Christ in order for the Father to be glorified in the Son. How can they believe these things? Why can't they not be normal? Why can't they be satisfied with attending church services once a week? Why can't they be satisfied with a move here and there . . . a twitch, a jerk and a jingle . . . a shake, a dance and a shout? Why can't they be satisfied with a clap and a little bit of noise?

68

* Why do they demand more?
* Why do they desire more?
* Why do they anticipate more?

Above all things, why are they willing to die for more? Not for more experiences, but for more of Him.

They wait. And they are coming out, for the third day has arrived. The day of the great release has fallen upon them. These strange ones, these folk, these believers, have a name: **The Third Day worshipers have arrived.**

They are willing to die not just for more of Him, but for all of Him.

These Third Day worshipers live and run and walk. They talk and breathe. **They preach and pray and worship. They read and study and grow. They disciple with principles different from those of the first and second day.** They use:

* **Principles that guide and lead them**
* **Principles that build and edify them**
* **Principles of empowerment, enrichment, enhancement and enjoyment**
* **Principles of utter and complete holiness**

Arise, I say, arise. Wait no longer, for the time has come; the time is now.

* **I speak to you, Third Day worshiper, arise.**
* **I speak to you, Third Day warrior, arise.**
* **I speak to you, Third Day Jesus freak, arise.**
* **I speak to you, Third Day woman, arise.**
* **I speak to you, Third Day man, arise.**
* **I speak to you, Third Day youth, arise.**
* **I speak to you, Third Day elder, arise.**

69

Your hour has come. Your hour of destiny has arrived. No longer do you need to be hidden. Your time of glory in His presence . . . of basking in the fullness of His might . . . has arrived. You have been hidden in the cave for so long. It is your time to enjoy the fullness of His power.

They wait no more; they wait no longer. They have arrived. The Third Day worshipers have arrived.

A number of underlying principles exist to enrich, enhance and empower Third Day worshipers. Principles are the bedrock . . . the solid foundation . . . the execution of the Third Day anointing. Principles connect and unite Third Day worshipers. These principles are fundamental truths. They are sound doctrines that have spearheaded us, that have led us into the third day. Principles to be followed without question, without compromise.

In the third day, we may praise and worship differently. The intensity in the volume may be magnified. The prophetic and the anointing, the signs, wonders and miracles, will be greater than in the first or second day. In His presence we have been revived, lifted up and made to live in His sight. Therefore, we will see greater things in the third day than any other day in history.

The sound doctrines . . . the tenets of our faith . . . the fundamental truths that guide the body of Christ in every way . . . are without compromise in the third day. These foundation truths reveal our one true God, Creator of the heavens and earth, manifested in the Trinity—the Father, the Son and the Holy Spirit. These truths hold up the Bible—the inspired, infallible Word of almighty God. They reveal the Lord Jesus Christ—

The third day is led by underlying principles that enable us to go further than the Christian generations prior to us.

70

fully God, the Son of God, always in existence. Our foundation truths teach us of the Fall of mankind and give the hope of the salvation of mankind. The basic ordinances of the church include the baptism in the Holy Spirit with its initial evidence of speaking in tongues. Through these foundation truths we understand sanctification, the church, divine healing, the blessed hope and the reign of Christ.

These are the basic fundamental principles to which we adhere. These go without compromise. They exist without question—regardless of what day we may be in.

Yet, in the third day there are other principles that lead us further into God.

THE PENTECOST PRINCIPLE: THREE TO THREE THOUSAND

Three to three thousand—let us call it the Pentecost principle. The principle of Pentecost goes way beyond a denominational interpretation of the experiences of the upper room. The principle of Pentecost deals with much more than the infilling and the baptism of the Holy Spirit. This principle from Pentecost is the principle of three to three thousand.

Let me explain. Peter denied Jesus three times, just as it was prophesied.

> *Jesus said to him, "Assuredly, I say to you that this night, before the rooster crows, you will deny Me three times."*
> —MATTHEW 26:34

Peter denied Jesus three times. Three times he negated his relationship with Him. Here we see Peter—a distraught, empty, forsaken individual. A man who at one moment proclaimed Jesus to be the Christ, the Anointed One, the Son of the living God. Peter denied Jesus. Peter—the same Peter who lifted up a sword to protect his Master—denied Jesus three times.

71

But something happened after the Resurrection. Something happened in the upper room.

> *But Peter, standing up with the eleven, raised his voice and said to them, "Men of Judea and all who dwell in Jerusalem, let this be known to you, and heed my words."*
> —ACTS 2:14

The principle of Pentecost will take you beyond a shout or a dance, loud services or hollers or screams. These are great things; we need more dancing, shouting and rejoicing in the church. But I believe that we have been too methodical. In the second day we were undeniably limited by the very parameters that, at one point, we were preaching in favor of.

The same Peter who denied Jesus three times stood up.

We became so theological in our mind-set, so rational, reasonable, humanistic, so intellectually inclined, that at times we denied the supernatural glory of God. We became so methodical, so programmed, so orderly in our own order and structure that we did not permit the Spirit of God to have His way in many of our lives, churches and services.

Pentecost is infilling; it is empowerment to preach the Word of God with boldness, signs, wonders and miracles.

72

Not just preaching the Word, but preaching it with an anointing. And not just any anointing, but with a supernatural anointing. It is preaching the gospel of Jesus *with* Jesus, *in* Jesus, *through* Jesus, *because* of Jesus. You can preach the gospel alone, or you can preach the gospel under the anointing of Jesus with the empowerment and baptism of the Holy Spirit.

✳ **When you come to the feet of Jesus Christ initially and accept Him as personal Lord and Savior, Christ enters into your heart.**

✳ **But the moment you are baptized into the Holy Spirit, you enter into the heart of God.**

That is the difference. Friend, the baptism of the Holy Spirit is a powerful experience. All Third Day worshipers need to be baptized with the baptism of the Holy Spirit. Not for salvation—but for survival, success and excellence.

It is impossible to fight off the works of the devils, principalities and governors of the air with only our theology and liturgical manifestations. We need to fight and defeat the enemy of darkness with the power of the Holy Spirit. There is no other distinguishing mark that will differentiate.

We need a fresh baptism, a fresh awakening and a fresh move of the Holy Spirit. The Third Day worshiper is in love, entangled and intertwined completely with the person of the Holy Spirit. It is the principle of three to three thousand. Let me further explain that to you. Peter denied Jesus three times. In the Book of John, Jesus confronted Peter after his denials.

So when they had eaten breakfast, Jesus said to Simon Peter, "Simon, son of Jonah, do you love Me more than these?" He said to Him, "Yes, Lord; You know that I love You." He said to him, "Feed My lambs." He said to him again a second time, "Simon, son of Jonah, do you love Me?" He said to Him, "Yes, Lord; You know that I love You." He said to him, "Tend my sheep." He said to him the third time,

73

*"Simon, son of Jonah, do you love Me?"
Peter was grieved because He said to him
the third time, "Do you love Me?" And he
said to Him, "Lord, You know all things;
You know that I love You." Jesus said to
him, "Feed My sheep . . . follow Me."*
—JOHN 21:15–17, 19

Jesus tells Peter three things: Fish, feed and follow. Jesus asked him, "Do you love Me, Peter?" Interestingly enough, Jesus asked Peter this question three times. And Peter replied every time.

I imagine every time Jesus questioned him, the intensity of Peter's voice reverberated with a rhetorical gesture of frustration until the final moment— the breaking point—when the true purpose of the Master's questions became apparent. That truth was revealed to Peter in the upper room. There Peter reconciles.

God works best with those who know the grace of Jesus Christ.

Peter gathered with one hundred twenty people in the upper room. And then his moment of truth happened. Whom did Jesus Christ choose to be the first Spirit-filled preacher in the very first Spirit-filled, Charismatic, Full Gospel, Pentecostal—whatever you would call it— Third Day crusade?

* **He could have chosen John who, arguably, failed Christ the least.**

* **He could have chosen Mary who anointed His feet with costly perfume.**

But He chose the one who denied Him. Why did He choose Peter rather than anyone else?

Once you know and experience firsthand the grace of Jesus Christ, you are a legitimate Third Day worshiper. The grace of Jesus Christ . . . the grace of God . . . the grace of the Almighty makes you a Third Day worshiper. The grace of Jesus upon the life of an individual is the greatest mystery in and of the ages. How God can have so much mercy upon humanity, how God can relate with fools and freaks is truly a mystery of grace. That is the principle that enabled Peter to stand up and preach.

> For every day of defeat, there will be one thousand days of victory.

The result of Peter's preaching? Three thousands souls came to Christ. Wait a moment! Stop! Contemplate, listen and look—stop! Look at the revelation again. Peter denied Jesus three times. And in his first message he reaped three thousand souls. He failed Jesus three times, yet he reaped three thousand souls. Here is the principle.

* **For every day of sickness, there will be one thousand days of health.**

* **For every day of suffering, there will be one thousand days of laughter.**

* **For every day of mourning, there will be one thousand days of dancing.**

* **For every day of sin, there will be one thousand days of holiness.**

That is one of the Third Day principles. It is the principle of Pentecost—the principle of three to three thousand.

* **For every day that you were down and out, there will be one thousand days when you will be on top.**

75

* For every day that you did not have money even for milk for your children, there will be one thousand days when you will be able to bless the children of others.

* For every day that you were rejected, there will be one thousand days when God will accept you.

* For every day you have been destroyed, there will be one thousand days when you will be built up and edified in His glory.

This is the principle of three to three thousand. Peter denied Christ three times, and he reaped three thousand souls. I can imagine what it would be like to interview Peter. Who is this man? I would call him, "Pentecost Man." This man represents the Third Day man and woman—Pentecost man and Pentecost woman.

I am not referring to a denominational or group label. I am referring to the experience of the upper room, of the great outpouring of the Holy Spirit with tongues of fire that sat upon them. God is about to sit upon each and every one of us in the third day. And when God sits upon us, friend, He crushes us. When God sits upon us, it is the opposite of what happened with Jacob.

76 Jacob fought with God and would not let go until God gave him the blessing. But in the third day, God fights with you, and He will not let you go until He blesses you.

* God will not let you go until He anoints you.

* God will not let you go until He lifts you up.

* God will not let you go until He elevates you.

✳ **God will not let you go until He takes you to the place of the fullness of glory, victory and might.**

I can imagine what would have happened that day in the upper room if CNN had interviewed Peter. They would have called him aside right after that first message when three thousand souls were saved. And they would ask him questions. "Wait a minute, sir. Let us interview you for a moment. Aren't you the one who walked on water?"

And Peter would reply, "I no longer need to walk on water, because now I have living water running through me."

Then they would ask, "Aren't you the one who lifted up the sword and cut off the ear of the soldier in order to protect your Master?"

Peter would answer, "I no longer need to lift up that sword to cut off the ear of the enemy, because I have a greater sword to cut off the head of the devil."

"What do you mean, sir?" they would ask in surprise.

And boldly, Pentecost Peter would respond, "I have the sword of the Spirit, the Word of the almighty God. Why cut off the ear when I can eliminate the entire head of the enemy? What I did was then, but this is now."

Still the reporter questions more: "Aren't you the one who denied Him three times before the rooster crowed?"

And Peter says, "Yes, that was I. Yet that was then, but this is now. When the rooster crowed, when the cock gave out the last holler, I had denied Christ three times. But when the Lamb lifted up the last sound, I was redeemed. Greater than the holler of the rooster, greater than the crow of the cock, were the shout and the whisper of the Lamb of Glory. That Lamb did more for me than any rooster or cock could ever do. When the rooster crowed, I was finished. But when the Lamb spoke, I just began."

77

That is the power of the principle of three to three thousand. **It is your time, my friend.** It is your time to declare your principle. It is your time to be lifted up. **It is your time to stand up and say, "I want my principle." It is time for your blessing.**

* **For every day you went through hell, there will be one thousand days where you will be walking in heaven.**

* **For every day of misery, one thousand days of celebration will be given to you.**

* **For every day of loneliness, one thousand days of being surrounded by those who love you will be released unto you.**

Your time has come. Your time has come to arise. It is time for you to stand up and declare this is your day. This is your Third Day principle. You are not just any man or woman; you are Pentecost man, and you are Pentecost woman.

* **You are faster than a speeding demon.**

* **You are more powerful than a lying devil.**

* **You are able to leap sin in a single bound.**

* **You are not a bird, although you have wings of eagles.**

* **You are not a plane, although you go from glory to glory.**

78

Our world today craves heroes. Our society is totally encircled and controlled by the imagery from the mass media that depicts what it believes a hero to be. We have athletes who have been made into sports heroes. We have heroes made out of political figures. Hollywood creates heroes. The media creates heroes of every context.

But let me tell you about the true heroes. The true heroes are the men and women of the third day. These are greater than Superman or Batman—greater than any other hero. These are people redeemed by the blood of the Lamb who, through the precious blood of Jesus Christ, withstand the onslaught of devils, demons, principalities and sin daily. These are the heroes of the third day. They are unashamed. They preach the gospel of Jesus Christ and dare to reach those who have never been reached. They dare to stretch out—to worship where there is no worship, to shout out when they have been told to be silent. These heroes arise with an incomparable anointing. They are Pentecost man and Pentecost woman.

Peter was the first Pentecost man. Peter stood up, reaping three to three thousand. One might argue, why this man who denied Christ? Why him?

* **If your praise goes up, His presence comes down.**
* **If your worship goes up, His glory comes down.**
* **If your prayer goes up, His anointing comes down.**

When Moses lifted up his hand, victory came down. The psalmist understood this truth:

I will lift up my eyes to the hills—from whence comes my help? My help comes from the LORD, who made heaven and earth.—PSALM 121:1–2

What goes up must come down. This is not a principle of Isaac Newton, but the principle of the Word of God.

Lift up your heads, O you gates! And be lifted up, you everlasting doors! And the King of glory shall come in. —PSALM 24:7

Arise, and the King of glory shall come in. Who is this King of glory? Jehovah God, strong and mighty. He is the King of glory.

THE LEADERSHIP PRINCIPLE

The second Third Day principle is the John the Baptist leadership model principle. This principle explains that although Christians in the first and second day have done many great things, we have failed in many other things. In the second day there came great distress, anxiety, confusion and disappointment along with the great increase, empowerment and growth. This occurred because we were not rooted with solidifying principles such as the John the Baptist leadership model principle.

Let me explain. For so long we have built our own empires and our own worlds.

* **Many have utilized the gospel for their own benefit.**

* **Many have utilized charisma for their own benefit.**

80

* **Many have utilized the anointing and have exploited it for personal benefits and gain.**

Unfortunately, those having done so—and doing so—have stained and compromised the gospel of Christ, which we are preaching at this hour.

The fact is that we were building kingdoms for ourselves rather than building God's kingdom.

We competed with one another. The body of Christ competes daily, hourly, as if the church were a micro-cosmic example or an extension of a capitalistic society in a capitalistic world. Capitalism may very well be the best economic system in the world today. But it is not the foundation of biblical teaching. We must not be compet-itive with one another—churches competing against each other, ministries against ministries, men and women of God against other men and women of God, worshiper against worshiper.

This first and second day spirit—more of a second day spirit, a spirit enhanced, motivated and induced by mass media and great communication systems—is detrimental to the church. This spirit of competitiveness has been a destructive cancer in the body of Christ. The fact that we need to remove this cancer from the body of Christ in the third day goes without question. The surgical procedures we utilize need to be examined. The John the Baptist lead-ership model principle explains and executes the very truths that will enable us to create successful churches, ministries, Christian organizations and, above all things, relationships.

* The Third Day church is not about programs.

* The Third Day church is not about min-istries.

* The Third Day church is not about organi-zations.

* The Third Day church is not about one man or one woman monopolizing the spotlight.

* The Third Day church is not about our name.

The Third Day church is about the name above all names, Jesus Christ!

The Third Day church is not about religion, but relationships. The Third Day church is based upon relationships, mutual acceptance, camaraderie, fellowship, transparency and integrity. **The Third Day church is a relationship-filled church. Relationship with God; relationships with one another. It is a church that builds relationships with individuals, communities, neighborhoods, arenas and areas. That is the Third Day church.** How does one measure true success in Christianity?

True success is not measured by the things you do in a moment; it is measured by the relationships you build and the legacy you leave behind.

By legacy, I don't mean the self-glorification or self-gratifying of one's ministry and actions. Legacy is whom you leave behind to take things further, deeper and higher, from glory to glory. John the Baptist said it best.

> *I indeed baptize you with water unto repentance, but He who is coming after me is mightier than I, whose sandals I am not worthy to carry. He will baptize you with the Holy Spirit and fire.*—Matthew 3:11

John the Baptist pointed to Jesus. Jesus pointed to us.

> *Most assuredly, I say to you, he who believes in Me, the works that I do he will do also; and greater works than these he will do, because I go to My Father.*—John 14:12

What a powerful teaching, truth and revelation. If we all would apply this principle in our lives, we would all turn our lives upside down in order to turn the world upside down. If we were to ask the Holy Spirit, "What is Your number

82

one priority right now?", would it be reaping a great harvest? Would it be extending more ministries? What is the number one priority in God's heart in the third day?

I believe the priority of the Holy Spirit in the third day is to prepare the church for His coming.

Friend, I believe that in the third day, even though the reaping of souls, the reaping of the masses, is in the heart of God, I do not believe this is the priority of the Holy Spirit at this hour.

The priority of the Holy Spirit in the third day is to prepare the bride for the return of the Bridegroom. It is to prepare us for the wedding feast of John 2.

> *On the third day there was a wedding in Cana of Galilee.—JOHN 2:1*

God is preparing us for that wedding. Therefore, we must change.

* Our views must change.
* Our concepts must change.
* Our ideas must change.
* Our formational relationships must change.
* Our structures must change.

The reason so many denominations fail is because they have safeguarded tenets and principles other than those found in the Word. They regarded bylaws and procedures as greater than individuals. We need to value people. We need to value individuals. God uses people—men and women of God. **God uses simple men and women.** If we learn to appreciate . . . to admonish . . . to acknowledge . . . **to recognize . . . to lift up . . . to use . . . to help . . . to assist . . . to serve one** another . . . **we will revolutionize the church and the body of Jesus Christ.** I do not want my name in neon lights in the third day. In the third day the moment will come when things will be much different than in any other day. In the third day, a powerful reality will exist, and many of us will be lifted up by this anointing.

> *After two days He will revive us; on the third day He will raise us up, that we may live in His sight.*—HOSEA 6:2

We will be raised up. We will reach masses around the world.

There will be two different types of armies.

✳ **An army that will function as revivers and resurrectors who will go into churches and into Christian arenas, into the body of Christ, to revive, arise and provoke all to live in God's holy sight.**

✳ **An army that will go out into the streets and into the world to reach the unsaved, to reach the lost and the backslidden, bringing them to the feet of Jesus Christ.**

When this happens, no longer will our names matter. No longer will we desire to have our names in neon lights. No longer will spearheading massive ministries around the world lift us up—rather God will lift us up. I pray that the day will arrive when Third Day men and women like you and I will function differently from those of the second day. We will no longer create empires around personalities, charisma and individual interpretations. We will go into countries and neighborhoods. Let the day come when we preach in cities, stadiums and arenas . . . when we reach one hundred thousand people with great miracles never seen before . . . with an anointing never experienced before. And at the end of the road, all we have is Jesus. And all we do is glorify Jesus.

 * Not rhetorically or psychologically, trying to convince ourselves that that is what we are doing

 * Not with articulated expressions giving all the glory and honor to God—when in reality we glorify and enhance ourselves and place ourselves on the altars

Rather, wholeheartedly we are hidden under the shadow of His wings as His light and glory reach all, cover all and shine upon all.

> All we do is build the stage; we lift Him up, and then we get out of the way and let Him be God.

Friend, the apostle Paul was a tentmaker. In the third day we are pulpit and stage makers. We make stages and pulpits. But for whom? Not for ourselves. We make them for Jesus.

We must be different. Many of the great spiritual fallouts we experienced in the second day came because we permitted the creating of one's own empire and kingdom to dominate the body of Christ. This act does not distinguish us from politicians, actors, actresses, movie stars or those who desire accolades.

85

 * Whether or not they clap for you,
 * whether or not they recognize you,
 * whether or not your name appears in neon lights,
 * whether or not you are on the cover of magazines,
 * whether or not you are invited to great events,

... regardless, you have an anointing and a calling to execute the Word of almighty God. For you are third day.

> The true measure of your success will be whom you leave behind. If whom you leave behind is greater than you, then you are truly third day.

As a Third Day pastor, if God calls me out of my church, my number one objective should be to leave someone behind me who is greater than me. As a youth supervisor of more than three hundred churches for ten years, supervising thousands of Christian young people in the northeast of the United States of America, my primary objective in my departure was to leave someone behind who would do greater things for the kingdom of God. That person could not be equal to me. That person must be greater than myself. If that person is equal to myself, then I have failed.

If those who follow me are greater than me . . . if the preachers and teachers to whom I preach and teach become greater preachers and teachers than me . . . If my congregation is greater . . . if my children are greater than their daddy . . . if they accomplish more for the glory of God . . . if they reach further . . . if they go to the next level . . . If they go deeper in the river of revival . . . then I have done an excellent job for Christ and through Christ.

* In the first and second day, we were greater than our students.
* But in the third day, our students will be greater than us.

We must follow the John the Baptist leadership model. He who follows me must be greater than me. When we follow that model, then we understand that we cannot build ourselves. This is an underlying principle of the Third Day worshiper. You and I are master servants, and our job is

Our job is to build relationships.

to serve, edify, enrich, enhance and empower those around us. Our job is to be Jesus to those around us.

❋ **Our job is not to build ministries.**
❋ **Our job is not to build organizations.**
❋ **Our job is not to build churches.**
❋ **Our job is not to build denominations.**

Jesus built relationships with twelve men, and as a result we are here today. In the third day, we will build relationships.

THE TWO BY TWO PRINCIPLE

Another powerful principle, principle number three, is the principle of two by two.

> *After these things the Lord appointed seventy others also, and sent them two by two before His face into every city and place where He Himself was about to go.*—LUKE 10:1

The Bible tells us that Jesus sent His disciples out two by two. Why aren't we going out two by two? Two key words for agile organizations in the twenty-first century are partnering and networking. These phrases are overused at times in the common market and in technology information access systems or aggressive organizations that are bringing transformation in the corporate world.

In the third day, we will not work alone; we will work two by two.

We must partner in the body of Christ. We must come together in the body of Christ. This is not a

87

matter of compromising one's convictions. We cannot compromise. But we must network and partner with other believers who believe in Jesus Christ, in the power of the cross of Calvary and in the empty tomb. We must do everything two by two.

* **It goes beyond prayer partners.**
* **It goes beyond accountability partners.**

Prayer partners and accountability partners are relevant, practical and applicable. But it goes beyond that. In Staten Island, New York, where I pastor, we needed to purchase vans because of an incredible growth that God has permitted us to experience. The church we founded with approximately ninety-two people had grown to nearly fifteen hundred worshipers in a matter of two years. Resources were scarce and limited. Yet we needed more vans to pick up those all over the city who desired to come to experience God's precious move and anointing.

> We are not building our church. We are building His church, His kingdom, His body.

But the Lord told me that first I needed to purchase a vehicle for another nearby ministry, one that needed transportation just as we needed it. So we bought for someone else. We gave away in order to acquire a van for our own ministry. Now you may call that foolishness. No, my friend, we understand the principle that we are not building our own empire.

We must go beyond annual community-wide services, rallies and gatherings. We must unite together to pray, worship, intercede and network in order to be revived, raised up and living in His sight. We must go forth two by two. God gave us that principle—one we must follow.

* **Moses had Aaron.**
* **Elijah had Elisha.**
* **David had Jonathan.**
* **Jesus had John.**
* **Paul had Timothy.**

We have the Holy Spirit. But we need to partner up with someone else in ministry. Pastor, I encourage you to partner up with another pastor. Worshiper, woman of God, I encourage you to partner up with another woman of God and come in agreement.

> *Again I say to you that if two of you agree on earth concerning anything that they ask, it will be done for them by My Father in heaven. For where two or three are gathered together in My name, I am there in the midst of them.*—MATTHEW 18:19–20

THE LIVING FOR HIM VS. DYING FOR HIM PRINCIPLE

Another powerful principle is the principle of living for Him vs. dying for Him. In the second day, we praised God for all who were willing to die for Him. In the first and second day, many died for the cause of Christ. That martyr spirit and anointing is legitimate in God's presence.

89

> *For to me, to live is Christ, and to die is gain.*—PHILIPPIANS 1:21

> *For if we live, we live to the Lord; and if we die, we die to the Lord. Therefore, whether we live or die, we are the Lord's.*
> —ROMANS 14:8

I believe in these truths. But there is a difference between dying for Christ and living for Christ.

* In the second day, we were willing to die for Him.
* But in the third day, we must be willing to live for Him.

In the third day, living is much more difficult than dying.

In the third day, dying is the easy way out. It is the escape from despair, anxiety, fear, confusion, ambiguity, desperation, hurt and pain—the feel of living. But those who live are the courageous ones. Those who live, in essence, are the ones who are dying. For those who live are dying to themselves daily. In the third day, the question is not whether you are willing to *die* for Jesus. The question is whether you are willing to *live* for Jesus.

> God is no longer asking you to be willing to die for Him. God is asking you to be willing to live for Him.

* A Third Day worshiper lives for Jesus Christ.
* A Third Day worshiper dies to self for Jesus Christ.
* A Third Day worshiper exists for Jesus Christ.

The question, again, is not if you are willing to die for Him. The question is, Are you willing to live for Him?

THE PRINCIPLE OF THE SWEAT AND THE ANOINTING

Friend, listen to this revelation: When we are most in stress, we produce the greatest anointing.

When we are most tested, most stressed and most challenged, we produce the greatest anointing. The greatest

90

anointing comes from the greatest pressure, the greatest confrontation, the greatest tribulation and the greatest circumstance. The reason you are going through what you are going through right now is not merely because the devil wants to destroy you. More importantly, it is because God wants to produce a greater anointing out of you. In the third day, the outflow of circumstances and challenges in our lives is not an indication of what the devil is doing against us—it is an indicator of what God is doing for us and through us. We are not fixated with Satan's activities in our lives, but we are obsessed with God's work in our lives. The greater the sweat, the greater the anointing.

The principle of the sweat and the anointing was evident in the life of the apostle Paul. As he ministered to thousands while traveling the world on his missionary journeys, a great anointing was poured out of his life—even as he faced tremendous confrontations and challenges. At one point in his ministry, the principle of sweat and anointing is clearly evident. As great miracles poured out of his life, even the handkerchiefs he used to wipe the sweat from his brow were used as instruments to produce a miracle.

> *Now God worked unusual miracles by the hands of Paul, so that even handkerchiefs or aprons were brought from his body to the sick, and the diseases left them and the evil spirits went out of them.*—Acts 19:11–12

God may not use the handkerchiefs of His great Third Day army to produce a harvest of miracles. But He will certainly pour a great anointing upon the lives of radical, obsessed men and women of God who are determined to turn their worlds upside down for God.

THE PRINCIPLE OF SOMEWHERE IN THE MIDDLE

The last Third Day underlying principle is the principle I call Somewhere in the Middle. Jesus has always been somewhere in the middle—never to the left and never to the right. He was in the middle of the people of Israel as a cloud by day and a fire by night.

> And the LORD went before them by day in a pillar of cloud to lead the way, and by night in a pillar of fire to give them light, so as to go by day and night.—EXODUS 13:21

He was in the middle of the fiery furnace with Shadrach, Meshach and Abednego.

> Then King Nebuchadnezzar was astonished; and he rose in haste and spoke, saying to his counselors, "Did we not cast three men bound into the midst of the fire?" They answered and said to the king, "True, O king." "Look!" he answered, "I see four men loose, walking in the midst of the fire; and they are not hurt, and the form of the fourth is like the Son of God."—DANIEL 3:24–25

92

* He was in the middle of the den of lions with Daniel.

* He was in the middle of the wheel with Ezekiel.

* He was in the middle of the crowd when the woman with the issue of blood broke through the crowd and touched the hem of His garment.

✳ **He was in the middle of two crosses two thousand years ago.**

Never to the left; never to the right; always in the middle. Why in the middle? Because in the middle there is balance.

Jesus has always been, and will always be, in the middle of things.

If you are positioned to the left or to the right, you are not balanced. The Third Day worshiper is a balanced worshiper, a balanced believer and a balanced Christian. All things are balanced—the Word with worship, prayer with fasting, holiness with evangelism. All things balance for a Third Day worshiper. Jesus is always . . .

✳ **Somewhere between yesterday and today.**
✳ **Somewhere between today and tomorrow.**
✳ **Somewhere between falling and getting up.**
✳ **Somewhere between your silence and your shout.**
✳ **Somewhere between sin and perfect holiness.**
✳ **Somewhere between your praise and worship.**

Somewhere in the middle of a sad and dying world, there is a joyful, living church. Somewhere in the middle of drug addiction, prostitution, homosexuality, abuse, broken homes, terrorism, school shootings and gang violence, there is a living, reigning Jesus Christ! Somewhere in the middle of dead religions, manmade organizations, there is an army of Third Day warriors and worshipers. **Somewhere in the middle of urban warfare, there is Holy Spirit revival. Somewhere in the middle of New Age, psychics, Ouija**

93

boards and witchcraft, there is incomparable power in the name of Jesus Christ. **Jesus is always in the middle.**

Somewhere in the middle of your hell there is a set of keys waiting for you. Many ask, Why do Christians suffer? Why do believers suffer? But when we understand the principle of the middle, then we know that in the midst of our sufferings, Jesus is with us. He did not promise that we would never go through suffering. He said, "In the midst of it, there I shall be with you."

You who do not believe in God go through hell for nothing, but I go through hell for a reason.

> *Peace I leave with you, My peace I give to you; not as the world gives do I give to you. Let not your heart be troubled, neither let it be afraid.*—JOHN 14:27

Listen, friend; you may go through hell. Even the closest people to you may ask, "Why are you sick?" "Why did someone in your family perish?" "Why are you suffering?"

At the end of your hell, you find death. But at the end of my hell, I find the victory, and I walk out with a set of keys.

* **My sickness is better than your sickness.**
* **My disease is better than your disease.**
* **My trial is better than your trial.**

94

And why is that? Because Jesus is in the midst of my sickness. He is in the midst of my disease. He is in the midst of my trial. Jesus is in the midst of every circumstance, situation and condition. Why has God permitted these things in my life? Only He knows. But in the midst of it, there is a miracle.

* In the second day, we waited for miracles.
* In the third day, there are miracles waiting for us.

So I ask you finally. I ask you truthfully. Are you waiting upon God, or is God waiting upon you? When Jesus was resurrected, Peter and John ran to tell the world that He was alive. But in Acts 2, the Bible talks about a rushing, mighty wind, which means that the Holy Spirit rushed. *The Holy Spirit ran to tell you that you are alive!*

Are you Third Day?

Raise the Volume

The search began. *The search continued.* **The search is over.** The search for whom? The search for what? The search for worshipers. Not just any worshiper—but those who worship Him in spirit and in truth . . . true worshipers . . . Third Day worshipers. In the third day, there shall be a new song.

> *Oh, sing to the LORD a new song! For He has done marvelous things.*—PSALM 98:1

> *But the hour is coming, and now is, when the true worshipers will worship the Father in spirit and truth; for the Father is seeking such to worship Him. God is Spirit, and those who worship Him must worship in spirit and truth.*—JOHN 4:23–24

It has always been about worshiping—all the struggles, conflicts, fights, attacks, confrontations, divisions, perplexities, anxieties, fears, confusions and ambiguity. It has always been about worship. The Third Day worshiper will answer the cry. The Third Day worshiper will exemplify and personalize the response of the great search. In the third day, the search will be over. God will find the true worshipers, those who worship Him in spirit and in truth. To be a Third Day worshiper, we must understand that everything we go through—all our circumstances and surroundings . . . our Christian walk and faith . . . the great struggle between good and evil . . . between Satan and God . . . between Jesus and the enemy—has always been, is and will be about one thing.

* **Not about churches**
* **Not about ministries**
* **Not about numbers**
* **Not about popularity**

Greater than all of these is the struggle for one thing—worshipers.

THE BIRTH OF WORSHIP

The story of worship began a very long time ago, long before Creation could utter and clutter the minuscule sounds of life. It began . . .

* **before the first breath,**
* **before the first song from a bird,**
* **before the falling of a leaf,**
* **before the roar of a lion,**
* **before the flow of a river,**
* **before the first cry of a child,**
* **before the moan of a dying adult.**

98

Before anything, there existed one powerful truth: God in the midst of eternity searching for worshipers.

So He created the angels, and as He created them, the first glimpse of worship appeared. A shadow of that which was to come. *Holy, holy, holy; holy is the Lord God Almighty. The earth is full of Your glory. Holy is the Lord.* Worship filled the ears of the great Master, the great

Father, the great Creator, the great Director of the most powerful orchestra yet to be heard.

Still God longed for more, so He created trees, rivers and mountains. Each sang a unique song of praise. To these sounds of praise God added the sound from each animal He created—until a symphony of praise arose from all of nature. To this day, nature praises and acknowledges the very existence of the sovereign Creator of the universe.

> Creation was created to worship, nothing more and nothing less.

But God desired more—much more. He desired worshipers who would utilize free will as the violin of their expression . . . who would look . . . reflect . . . who would *be* the image of the perfect song and the perfect sound. So God searched again, and God created man in His image. All of Creation is about worship.

All of Creation exists to acknowledge and recognize the very being of Him who created all things.

But after all was said and done, yet He anguished and desired one thing—*a worshiper like Him.* That He had not yet seen. So at that moment something happened. At that moment man was created to sing the song of the Lord, to lift up the name of God, to worship. The worshiper began to worship. And the song was being played.

99

THE WAR OF WORSHIP

But it must be understood that something had happened before. In the midst of the first great anthem of praise that arose from the angels in heaven, at the moment of initial worship in the heavenlies, a great war occurred. It was there that the angel of light, Lucifer . . . he who orchestrated and organized the first ensemble . . . who led the praise and worship . . . that great praise and worship leader of the heavens . . . began to sing a song that God Jehovah could never hear, a song that could never be tolerated in the ears of the sovereign Master of music. It was

* a song of dissension,
* a song of division,
* a song of jealousy,
* a song of strife.

God had never heard that song before. When that song was played and the melody was presented, there was no other choice but to reject the worship and the evil worshiper. He was rejected and cast out upon the earth. When he came, he brought with him those who worshiped with him and like him. Part of the great praise and worship ministry of the heavenlies was cast out because they sang the wrong song.

Satan declared a war against one thing, true worship.

When God created man in His image and likeness, God was pleased with His new worshipers. Adam worshiped Him. Eve worshiped Him. But then it happened again. Satan declared a war.

* Not a war against organizations,
* not a war against ministries,
* not a war against churches,
* but a war against true worship.

And so the war began. Satan wrote a song upon the souls of men that had never been written before. Satan wrote the song of dissension. He wrote the song of division. He wrote the song of abortion and homosexuality. He wrote the song of perversion, fear, lust and suicide.

✳ Satan wrote the song of abuse and abandonment upon a minor child.

✳ To this day, he writes the song of suicide
and abuse on women throughout the world.

✳ Upon the forty-three-year-old Wall Street
banker, he writes a song of torture, loneliness, insecurity and complexes.

✳ Upon that fifteen-year-old young woman, he
writes the song of sexual promiscuity.

✳ Upon the soul of that twenty-two-year-old
college graduate, he writes the song of
agnosticism.

✳ Upon the souls of millions in the Middle East
and throughout the world, he writes the song
of false religion, the occult and New Age.

✳ Upon the souls of Christians across America
and across the world, he wrote the song of
religion, comfort, man-made dogmas, division, strife, anarchy and chaos.

✳ Upon the souls of men he writes, until mankind overflows with bitterness, hatred, dis-
sent, confusion, anger and malice.

He is continually writing upon the souls of men. It is a
song of worship—to death, hell, annihilation, utter
destruction—worship to him. Satan, the enemy of
God—and ours—descended upon the face of the earth
and wrote upon the souls of men.

God the Father, surrounded by the group of angels
singing, "Holy, holy, holy," became overwhelmed by the

Who will arise to write a new song? Who will arise? sound coming from mankind, whom He had created in His image to worship Him in spirit and in truth. What a challenge, what a struggle. In one ear came the sounds of "holy, holy, holy." In the other ear He heard the cries of desperation, death and destruction from His children.

* **Pain was the melody in the chorus.**
* **Destruction was the stanza.**
* **Sin was the major note.**

He listened until the moment He could listen no longer.

JESUS, THE SONGWRITER

As tears streamed down the cheeks of the almighty Creator, He asked who would write a song that all of creation could sing. God the Father exclaimed, "I need someone.

* **"I need someone who will descend.**
* **"I need someone who will arise.**

"I need someone who will write a new song . . . a song to silence the song that was written by the enemy . . . a song to annihilate and erase the words and lyrics written upon the souls of My worshipers—those formed in My image to worship Me in spirit and in truth."

Then Abraham came to Him and said, "I will write a new song to You, God."

And God said, "Tell Me, what is your song?"

And Abraham said, "I will write to You the song of the covenant."

And God replied, "That song would not be sufficient, Abraham. I need someone to write Me a new song."

102

Moses came and said, "Father, I will write a new song."

"Moses," God asked, "what is the name of your song?"

And Moses said, "I will call it the Law."

The Father responded, "The Law will not be sufficient for freeing My true worshipers."

Then came David, who said, "I will write Your song."

God responded, "David, you are My king. You are My psalmist. You are My poet. If there is anyone who can write Me a song, you should be able to write Me a song. Give Me the song, David."

So David sang Him the song of Israel and of Jerusalem, the song of the monarchy, the song of royalty, the song of the unified kingdom. But that song was not sufficient. God said, "David, that song will not liberate the worshiper. That song will not overcome the song written by the enemy. I need a new song."

Meanwhile, the angels cried, "Holy, holy, holy." And as they sang, a sound arose above their noise—a contradictory chorus. The cry of humanity inundated the heavenly places in the ears of God, imploring, "Help me, help me, help me, Lord! Why have You forsaken me? My bones, crushed and weary, will never be able to praise You."

Overwhelmed by the cry of His children, God arose. Crying out, He said, "I need someone to write Me a new song."

103

* **Who will write the song?**
* **Who will compose the song?**
* **Who will orchestrate the song?**
* **Who will sing the song?**

All the prophets—Isaiah, Jeremiah, Ezekiel, Daniel, Hosea, Joel, Amos, Obadiah, Jonah, Micah, Nahum, Habakkuk, Zephaniah, Haggai, Zechariah and Malachi—all of them presented songs onto the Lord. But none of them could free the worshipers. None of them could accomplish the task.

For four hundred years, no one dared to present a song before the throne of God. As Satan escalated his war—the war of worship—he wrote the final stanzas and choruses to the songs of humanity. As he wrote, the cry of humanity intensified. In desperation, the Lord cried out, "Is there anyone who will be able to write Me a new song?"

And then it happened. Touching the back of the Father like a child pulling on the hem of his father's coat, there was One who said, "Father, I shall write You a new song!" Jesus arose and said, "Let Me write You the new song."

And the Father looked at the Son and said, "Son, do You know what this means?"

And the Son said, "Yes, Father. I and only I can write the new song." And Jesus descended to begin His song.

Here is the Man who has never been recognized by the music industry.

✱ **He never received a Grammy award.**

✱ **He never had a video on MTV.**

✱ **He never had a song or hymn published.**

✱ **He never sang in Carnegie Hall.**

✱ **He never was recognized by the great musicians, orchestras or symphonies of our time.**

Nevertheless, He is the greatest songwriter in the history of mankind.

Two thousand years ago, He began to write the song. Searching, He said, "I need to write on something." What do we normally write on? We write on paper. Paper comes from wood. He lifted up two pieces of wood in the form of a cross.

Then He said, "I need a utensil. I need to write with something." He picked up three nails.

Finally He said, "I need ink—not just any ink, but the kind that can never be washed away." The blood of Jesus Christ washes us of all of our sins. He became sin when sin He knew not.

> *For God so loved the world that he gave his one and only Son, that whoever believes in him shall not perish but have eternal life.*
> —JOHN 3:16, NIV

Jesus began to write a song—the song of deliverance, the song of freedom.

* The song of redemption
* The song of forgiveness
* The song of healing

Then you will know the truth, and the truth will set you free.—JOHN 8:32, NIV

So if the Son sets you free, you will be free indeed.—JOHN 8:36, NIV

105

He wrote the song of healing on that day two thousand years ago.

> *But he was pierced for our transgressions, he was crushed for our iniquities; the punishment that brought us peace was upon*

him, and by his wounds we are healed.
—ISAIAH 53:5, NIV

✳ **He wrote the song of miracles.**
✳ **He wrote the songs of destiny.**
✳ **He wrote the songs of utter joy.**

Jesus, the Songwriter, wrote the song on that day. Two thousand years ago, using the frequency of our faith, the tempo of our temple, the beat of our drum and the rhythm of the Resurrection, the Poet of Pentecost wrote the song.

And as He wrote, verse by verse, He wrote a song that replaced the song that was written upon the souls of humanity by the other one—the one who was the anathema to true worship. He wrote the song, crying out word by word. He wrote the verse of loneliness—perhaps the most powerful verse. This verse said, "I know what it is to be alone."

> You and I can never say, "God, You do not know what it is to be abandoned or forsaken."

On that day, two thousand years ago, the great Songwriter wrote the song of loneliness and abandonment. He asked, "Father, why has Thou forsaken Me?" He wrote it in a moment when complete and utter forsakenness descended upon this Master of song writing.

The Master of worship, with His new song, catapulted us into a guarantee that we would never have to be lonely. He was abandoned, so you and I could be carried . . . never forsaken . . . verse by verse by verse. He wrote the song until the final verse. As the blood flowed on that wooden cross, the songs of the enemy were washed away.

Jesus called out with a loud voice, "Father, into your hands I commit my spirit." When he had said this, he breathed his last.
—LUKE 23:46, NIV

He wrote, "It is finished. Into Thy hands I commit My spirit."

At the cross, at the cross where I first saw the light
And the burden of my heart rolled away—
It was there by faith I received my sight,
And now I am happy all the day![1]

THE SOUND GREATER THAN THE NOISE

Two thousand years ago, at three o'clock on a Friday afternoon, the music died for two days. Nothing was heard. Music was not sung from creation. Nature reacted to the crucifixion. Darkness overtook the face of the earth. Earthquakes shook the earth.

The songwriter was silenced with a musical pause that shortly would crescendo into the greatest example of worship in the history of Creation. For two days, the only sound that could be heard was the groan of the Father who had just lost His Son.

> The songwriter was silenced, not by man, but by His fathomless love.

But in the third day, something happened. The prophecy was fulfilled in the third day. The spirit of heaviness was removed, and the Father rose from the throne with the garment of praise, looked down at the tomb and said, "Son, raise the volume!"

107

* **The resurrection chorus began.**

* **The song of the redeemed was sung.**

* **The living song, the song of salvation, the new song was finalized.**

Jesus Christ had resurrected from the dead, hallelujah!

The song of eternal hope and eternal salvation was sung. As Jesus was resurrected, the devil and his symphony approached Him, the resurrected Songwriter of the new song. Not only did He write the song, now He sang the glorious song: "You have been redeemed; you have been washed by the blood of the Lamb."

Grimacing at the sound, the enemy asked, "What is this?"

And Jesus replied, "It is time for a new song. You have been singing your song. Your song has been heard throughout the generations. Now it is time for My song to be heard. My song is the sound of grace, the sound of forgiveness."

* **What does grace sound like?**
* **What does forgiveness sound like?**
* **What does redemption sound like?**

Arise, Third Day worshiper! Arise with the sound of grace! Arise with the sound of forgiveness! Arise with the sound of deliverance! Arise with the sound of holiness!

* **We need to go beyond the sounds of noise we made in the second day.**

* **We need to make a new sound in the third day.**

When the demons, devils and principalities in high places hear this song, they will have no other choice but to surrender to the song of glory. Everything created will begin to sing this song—and the thundering sounds of praise will invade the very throne room of God.

In this third day, there will be a song that has never been heard before.

Make a sound that is understood. Make a sound without ambiguity and confusion. Let it be a loud sound. I am tired of the whispers. I am tired of the introverted sound.

* A second day Christian prayed in the prayer closet, but a Third Day Christian prays through the windows.

* A second day Christian participated in praise and worship in the midst of the sanctuary with other believers, but a Third Day worshiper praises and worships in the bedroom . . . in the shower . . . in the car.

There will be a new song of revival, of raising up and living in God's sight.

I know that there are Christians who are radical enough to praise and worship everywhere at all times without hesitation. *Praise the Lord, all the inhabitants of the earth, and all the peoples. All that have breath, praised be the name of the Lord.* **Praise the Lord.** Tell your hands to praise Him. Tell your feet to praise Him. **Tell your back, your head, your ears, your nose, your eyes to praise Him. Tell your soul to praise Him. Tell your spirit to praise Him.**

The Bible says that He anoints our head with oil:

> *You anoint my head with oil; my cup overflows.*—PSALM 23:5, NIV

Why does God anoint our head with oil? Because in our head we have our eyes, our mouths, our ears and our nose.

* **We have vision.**
* **We have praise.**
* **We have worship.**

We have been created to praise the Lord. We are worshipers, and there is power in worship. Praise executes the vengeance of the Lord upon the enemy, while worship provokes the passion of the Lord upon His people.

* **We need to raise the volume at this hour.**
* **We praise to get the devil out of the way.**
* **We worship to bring God in the way.**

THE NEW WORSHIPERS

Our story continues:

As Satan stands before Jesus, he asks, "What are You going to do now?"

And Jesus says, "I have a new song. One that I am not going to sing alone."

"So, bring Your angels," Satan replies. "They have been singing for eons—I was part of them."

And Jesus replied, "Satan, I have news for you. The angels are not going to sing this song."

In surprise, Satan replied, "What are You talking about? They have always been the worshipers."

But Jesus responded, "I know, but now I have made an addition to the heavenly chorus. Now I have

* *a new band,*
* *a new orchestra,*
* *a new symphony,*
* *a new ensemble,*
* *a new group of worshipers."*

Satan replied, "That cannot be! What are You talking about? It has always been the angels. Tell the angels to sing it."

Jesus replied, "No, it is not the angels." Then He pointed to the new worshipers. They included

- *children redeemed by the precious blood of the Lamb,*
- *young people sealed with the Holy Spirit,*
- *adults filled with God's glory,*
- *elders equipped with God's armor.*

God points to you, my brother and my sister. He points to you, my fellow believer. He says, "Raise the volume, raise the volume! Let it be heard throughout the nations that Jesus Christ is Lord. Let it be heard throughout the nations."

✳ **Jesus saves.**
✳ **Jesus delivers.**
✳ **Jesus heals.**
✳ **Jesus baptizes.**

And He is coming back again. Jesus Christ is Lord! So I instruct you at this hour to raise the volume. Sing the new song. The first stanza was written by the Father—the song of Creation. The second was written in blood by the Son—the song of redemption. But then came the third verse. The third verse began to be written two thousand years ago when Jesus said, "I shall go, but I will send you the Comforter. And you shall receive power when the Holy Spirit comes upon you." Two thousand years ago in the upper room, the first Spirit-filled choir, a group of one hundred twenty people, sang forth the finished third verse—the song written by the Holy Spirit as He came to earth to be with us.

✳ **The Father wrote the song with His fingers.**
✳ **Jesus wrote the song with His hands.**
✳ **But the Holy Spirit wrote the song with fire.**

That is why this third verse makes me shout, jump, scream and dance. It is a fiery song. It is an indiscernible song. When He wrote the verse, we started to read it. But it cannot be read by humanity—and it cannot be read by the devil. It was not written in man's language; it was not written in an understandable language. Sure, parts of it were written in the languages of other people of the nations that were gathered in Jerusalem that day. But there is a language today that is being sung that the world cannot understand.

> It is the song of the third day, the song of the Spirit, the prophetic song of the Lord.

The congregation may not understand it . . . your friends and neighbors may not understand it. We need to sing this song in the Spirit.

> So what shall I do? I will pray with my spirit, but I will also pray with my mind; I will sing with my spirit, but I will also sing with my mind.—1 Corinthians 14:15, NIV

112

> Let the word of Christ dwell in you richly as you teach and admonish one another with all wisdom, and as you sing psalms, hymns and spiritual songs with gratitude in your hearts to God.—Colossians 3:16, NIV

The song of the Third Day worshiper is

- ✳ the song of the Holy Spirit,
- ✳ the song of the Lord,
- ✳ the song of power.

The hour has come for us to sing that song. The hour has come for the true worshipers to arise.

- ✳ We go beyond the music.
- ✳ We go beyond the noise.
- ✳ We go beyond the volume.

We go beyond controversy between contemporary Christian music and the old hymns. We need to go beyond these conflicts and confrontations.

You must get to the point of understanding that you are praise. You are the walking glory of God. Your life makes the sound.

We praise the Lord for the shofars that signaled praise in Bible times—and today. We praise the Lord for the utilization of these instruments in spiritual warfare. We recognize them as symbols of biblical authority, the sounding of the alarm in Mount Zion. But we are the true shofars.

We are the ram's horns that have been ripped and washed with blood and oil. Joshua, Moses and the prophets played the shofars in an earlier day. But it is the Holy Spirit of God who is lifting you up to His mouth and making the sounds of praise through your life. You are the shofar of the third day. I am the shofar of the third day. We are the song of this day. Rejoice when the Lord tells you to rejoice. We cannot be held back in the third day. In the third day we, the worshipers of the third day, will worship God in spirit and in truth without hesitation, restrictions, limitations and hindrances.

We need to sing in the Holy Spirit and to sing the song of the Lord.

113

A HEAVENLY SOUND

Grace makes a sound. Deliverance makes a sound. Healing makes a sound. What is that sound?

✳ **You are the sound of grace.**
✳ **You are the sound of deliverance.**
✳ **You are the sound of healing.**

Jesus Christ paid the price to write the song upon your life, to make a sound with your life. Therefore, make a joyful noise unto the Lord. We can make a noise unto the Lord because He will be able to understand the noise. God is able to distinguish and understand the noise. But we will not make a noise unto the world.

The sound we make must be clear before the world. It needs to be relevant. It needs to be transparent. It needs to be discernable. It needs to be understandable before the world. The sound coming from your life needs to be the sound of holiness, of integrity in the Word of God, of praying in the Spirit and with the Spirit. The song of the Lord is the prophetic song.

> A Third Day worshiper makes a sound unto the world and a noise before the Lord

It is the sound of a woman who dares to arise, to go out and to purchase a pair of new pants from Wal-Mart. As she begins to hem the pants, the next-door neighbor asks, "Why do you prepare those men's pants?"

And the woman replies, "These are for my son."

In surprise the neighbor replies, "But your son is in jail serving a life sentence."

And the woman replies, "You see him in jail serving a life sentence without knowing the Lord. But I see him being

114

baptized in water and being baptized in the Holy Spirit."

We need to write the prophetic song. We need to declare the things that are not as though they were.

❋ **The first verse was about Creation.**
❋ **The second verse was about redemption.**
❋ **The third verse is about empowerment.**

All three verses are being sung in the third day. But that third verse is being exemplified and exalted to a higher level. That third verse is being sung—and needs to be sung—by the church more and more on a daily basis. That song, that verse by the Holy Spirit, is a radical verse. It tells us—and the world—that not only are we sinners saved by grace, but we are saints empowered by His Spirit.

THE UNAVOIDABLE PROPHETIC VOICE

I was born in 1969 and raised in the city of Newark, New Jersey. We were a very tightly knit family. My grandparents were vital ingredients of our family. My grandfather, a minister from Puerto Rico, was the father of eleven children and the grandfather of nearly ninety grandchildren. He had a peculiar habit regarding me. No matter where we were, each time I greeted him, he would first say my name, and then he would speak in other tongues over me.

I did not understand this. As a teenager, there came a time when I was attempting to create relationships—especially with the opposite sex. I did not want to be in the middle of a gathering of people and have my grandfather start speaking aloud in tongues when I greeted him. I attempted to avoid him, but I would hear him call, "Samuel, come here." Then I would approach him and whisper, "Yes, Grandfather, I love you. It's good to see you." I was trying to deviate him from what I knew would follow.

Suddenly a roar would come from his mouth, and he would begin to speak in other tongues.

I was perplexed about this. Grandpa having the Holy Spirit was the most frightening thing in the world to me because he was not ashamed to express it. He would pray over people in tongues, releasing a prophetic word. He would do strange things, and now I understand why.

Now I understand why because the same things have evolved in me. One day when I took my first child to school, I paused to pray over my child. I began to do the same things with my children that my grandfather did with me as he prayed in the Holy Spirit. I had the same infectious disease that my grandfather had. I sang the same verse that he sang. It was that third verse by the Spirit—the song that we are singing now in our generation.

My friend, I tell you this. Be not afraid. Be not afraid. Be not afraid.

* **Be not afraid to function in the world of the Spirit.**

* **Be not afraid to function under the anointing.**

* **Be not afraid to function for the glory of God.**

* **Be not afraid to execute the word of the Lord.**

* **Be not afraid to flow in the anointing of God.**

* **Be not afraid to use the precious gifts of the Holy Spirit.**

Do not be afraid. *Do not be afraid.* **Do not be afraid.** We need to raise the volume in the third day.

* The music is different.
* Our language is different.
* The symphony is different.
* The stanza is different.
* The orchestra is different.
* The ensemble is different.
* The songs are different.

But nevertheless, it is the sound of grace. Grace has a sound. You are the sound of grace. Raise the volume.

Are you Third Day?

---

1. "At the Cross" by Isaac Watts; refrain, Ralph E. Hudson. Public domain.

Raise Up the Jesus Posse

Pharisee, *follower*, **freak**—everyone in the body of Christ falls under one of three labels. You are either a first day Pharisee, a second day follower or a Third Day freak.

The Pharisees were:

- ✳ **Upholders of tradition**—Mark 7:3, 5, 8
- ✳ **Sticklers for the law**—Acts 26:5
- ✳ **Preoccupied with outward detail**—Luke 18:11
- ✳ **Lovers of display**—Matthew 23:5–7
- ✳ **Persecutors**—Acts 9:1–2
- ✳ **Vipers**—Matthew 12:34
- ✳ **Blind**—Matthew 15:12–14
- ✳ **Hypocrites**—Matthew 23:13–19
- ✳ **Serpents**—Matthew 23:33
- ✳ **Children of the devil**—John 8:44

These are the Pharisees, the separated ones and the distinguished ones. Pharisees exist in the third day. Pharisees exist in churches, congregations and ministries, in our surroundings, in religious environments. Pharisees exist.

Pharisees uphold the traditions of men. Pharisees are more preoccupied with reserving and maintaining the status quo—the spirit of monotony and conformity—than with entering fully into the river of God's glory. Pharisees are more preoccupied with the Law—outward detail and display—than they are with grace and its undesirables—the brokenhearted and the disenfranchised. Pharisees exist in the third day.

✳ **God is not impressed with résumés.**

✳ **God is not impressed with theological backgrounds.**

✳ **God is not impressed with the cultural surroundings of society that elevate one person to a higher level than the other.**

You may not have a fan club, but you have the blood of Jesus Christ. You are either a first day Pharisee, a second day follower or a Third Day freak.

ONE OF THE THREE: THE FOLLOWERS

One may argue, saying, "I am not a Pharisee, but I may be a follower." Followers are those who *almost* touch Him, yet are satisfied with just being close to Him.

> It's not sufficient for you to follow Him just to be at His side. In the third day, you must be inside of Him and He inside of you.

When the woman with the issue of blood got the opportunity, she broke through a crowd to touch Jesus, and virtue came out of Him. The crowd was pressing Him, it surrounded Him, but it was not provoking virtue to come out of Him. When a woman with a need touched Him, she provoked virtue to come out of Christ.

CARRYING THE CROSS

Then He said to them all, "If anyone desires to come after Me, let him deny himself, and take up his cross daily, and follow Me."—LUKE 9:23

Christ never intended for us to carry the cross on our backs; He paid the price for us to carry the cross in our hearts.

The reason we are always dropping our cross is because we are carrying it the wrong way.

Because we attempt to carry the cross on the exterior, rather than the interior, we are continuously dropping our faith, our relationships and our anointing. Carrying the cross in our hearts involves

* ✳ **more than having a Jesus fish or a Jesus bumper sticker,**

* ✳ **more than wearing a WWJD bracelet or necklace,**

* ✳ **more than owning Christian T-shirts,**

* ✳ **more than carrying a big Bible,**

* ✳ **more than having contemporary Christian music playing in our car and workplace.**

121

It involves so much more. Such things are powerful as instruments of our testimony, but it is more important to carry the cross in our hearts than outside. As we carry the cross inside, we internalize our divine relationship with the Christ of the cross, with the reality of who He is. Wearing a cross inside, in our heart, and a crown on the outside will distinguish Third Day worshipers from those from the first and second days.

WOOD AND GOLD

The ark of the covenant was carried on sticks of wood and gold, perpetuating the reality of the glory of God being placed at a specific location and followed continuously. The ark was symbolic of the presence of God. It took four Levites to carry the glory. Four Levites who went through rituals, who went through ceremonies, who were prepared and separated all their lives to carry the ark of the covenant.

What four Levites could not do in the Old Covenant, one man washed in the blood of Jesus can do in the New Covenant.

But today, one individual washed by the blood of Jesus can carry the fullness of the glory of God.

That which four men carried in the Old Covenant can be carried by one man in the New Covenant.

* We carry more than the rod of Aaron.

* We carry more than the manna.

* We carry more than the Ten Commandments.

* We carry more than the paraphernalia.

* We carry more than the ceremonies and rituals.

We carry the fullness of the glory of God.

* We are the carriers of the glory.
* We are the Levites of the third day.

Above us we do not have cherubims covering our heads—we have the anointing of the Holy Spirit. The Third Person of the Trinity personally escorts us to carry the glory. We, the Third Day worshipers, carry the glory of God. Declare that you are carrying something.

In the second day, you carried your sins and problems, but in the third day, you carry the glory of God.

PARTAKERS OF THE DIVINE NATURE

Oh, my friends, we are partakers of His divine nature.

> *By which have been given to us exceedingly great and precious promises, that through these you may be partakers of the divine nature, having escaped the corruption that is in the world through lust.*—2 PETER 1:4

We are not spectators of His divine nature.

✳ **We partake . . .**
✳ **We interact . . .**
✳ **We participate . . .**
✳ **We consume His divine nature.**

123

We can walk into homes and declare that the glory of God is here! We need to go into neighborhoods and communities throughout our nation and shout forth the news that the glory of Jesus Christ has arrived!

Our expectations have to change; the way we approach things needs to change. We need to expect something to happen when we greet someone.

✳ **That person will be healed.**

✳ **That person will be delivered.**

✳ **That person will be transformed.**

✳ **That person will be baptized in the Holy Ghost and fire.**

Something needs to happen in the third day. We should expect that every time we come in contact with another human being, something will happen. A supernatural occurrence must be realized.

A THIRD DAY OCCURRENCE

A Third Day occurrence happened to me one day as I walked onto the second floor of the Lehigh Valley Mall in Allentown, Pennsylvania. I was accompanied by a number of youth pastors and leaders who were visiting for a youth conference that weekend. As we walked toward McDonald's—that infamous restaurant chain offering exquisite meals and classy decor—we passed two young women who were selling sweaters in a store located right next to McDonald's. We entered McDonald's and made our purchases. Suddenly one of the young women approached me and asked, "Can you come out here for a moment? We would like to speak to you."

Out in the mall area, I asked, "How may we help you?"

The young woman replied, "The assistant manager of our store has been unable to stop weeping since she saw you walk by earlier. I do not know who you are or what beliefs you have. I do not know anything about you. You may think this is strange, but the moment your group passed by her, she looked at you. Ever since that moment she has been crying."

RAISE UP THE JESUS POSSE

We approached the manager immediately and asked, "Is there anything we can do? How can we help you?"

All that she could say was, "It's you, it's you!"

"Did we do anything to offend you?" I asked.

"Oh, no, quite the contrary," she said. "As you passed by, I looked at your eyes. Something happened immediately in my heart. Something began to break. I began to hear a voice resonating in my spirit, inside of me, like a little voice telling me that I must get my life straightened out." She paused, and then continued, "Sir, I do not know if you are religious or not. I do not know who you are. You don't look like a religious person. You may think this is ludicrous, but there is something coming out of you that is making me question my relationship with God. I do not even go to church; I am not even a religious person, but something is making me think about God. This is the first time that this has happened to me."

I looked at her, and said, "Woman, you are not going through a nervous breakdown; this is not an abnormal experience. This is not something from your brain—this is the work of the Holy Spirit. The Spirit of God is within me. What you are experiencing is the reflection of Jesus Christ in my life. The Jesus inside of me is being poured out and is ministering to you. You need Jesus right now. What you are sensing is the convicting power of the Holy Spirit."

THE GLORY OF GOD

125

At all times, in all your Third Day experiences, the glory of God must be visible and active. For too long we have kept

> We must take the glory out God of the box and pour it upon this generation.

the blessings inside the walls; for too long we have maintained that the outpouring of God's glory was for churches and conventions and gatherings and religious arenas only.

We must pour the glory upon our cities, upon our neighborhoods, upon our communities, **upon our families, upon our friends and upon our enemies. We must pour out the glory.** We must pour out God's presence and anointing. We must be poured out completely every day. We must utilize all of our anointing before it becomes rotten.

Every day God pours out a fresh anointing upon your life. His blessings and His mercies are new every morning. His anointing upon your life is not for you to keep and store up somewhere—His anointing is for you to use. Every time you use it in its entirety, you come back to the throne room of grace before the Lord of glory. He gives you more anointing, fresh anointing.

As Third Day worshipers, we are more than first day Pharisees or second day followers—we are Third Day freaks. Jesus freaks can be found in so many churches in the third day. These fanatics never tire of praising, worshiping, celebrating and exalting the name of Christ. Sometimes our demand for order, control and structure causes us to misunderstand these people. At one time, Jesus freaks were in the pit of hell. They came out of the miry grave. They were alienated, confused and destroyed. But one day Jesus set them free.

126

Many of us who have been raised in the church have a hard time understanding what it means to be delivered—completely delivered—from the bondage of hell. A Jesus freak knows the power of God that frees him from the bondages of this world.

A Jesus freak is someone who has been brought out from the miry grave of sin. A Jesus freak has been delivered from the greatest of chains. Jesus freaks cannot say enough, praise enough, read enough, study enough and rejoice enough to celebrate the freedom that they have in

Christ Jesus. These Third Day freaks are a group of four distinguishable groups of people:

* **The upsetters**
* **The rejects**
* **The undesirables**
* **The unashamed**

This world has its witches, warlocks and drug addicts, but we have something greater—we have Jesus freaks. They are blood-washed, born-again and Spirit-filled— and proud of it. They are fanatics for Jesus Christ.

Jesus freaks: The upsetters

The upsetters represent the first group of freaks. We find them mentioned in Acts 17:6:

> *But when they did not find them, they dragged Jason and some brethren to the rulers of the city, crying out, "These who have turned the world upside down have come here too."*

Have you upset the devil today? More than a thousand demons may be trying to keep your hands down, but when you lift up your hands, you upset those thousand demons. A thousand devils may be trying to keep your mouth shut, but when you say one hallelujah, those devils are upset. The word *upset* is defined as "to force out of position, overturn, throw into disorder or to defeat unexpectedly." Praise forces the devil out of position...defeats him unexpectedly. When I praise, Hades closes its gates. The devil will never go to hell unless you begin to praise. Arise and upset the world. Arise and upset the devil. I am going to

* **upset religion,**
* **upset the devil with praise,**

127

* **upset the devil with a shout,**
* **upset the devil with joy,**
* **upset the devil with victory,**
* **upset the devil with zeal,**
* **upset the devil with perseverance,**
* **upset the devil with the Word,**
* **upset the devil with God's promises,**
* **upset the devil with the anointing.**

It is your time to upset the devil.

Jesus freaks: The rejects

There is a second group of Jesus freaks, a group that comprises the largest number of Jesus freaks. That group is known as the rejects. It includes:

* **The lepers**
* **The wounded**
* **The hurting**
* **The disenfranchised**
* **The alienated**

These are the rejects. Becoming a part of this group is not the result of a popularity contest—sooner or later everyone used by God will suffer rejection. Jesus was rejected and convicted. You may be rejected by the world. But you have been accepted by Jesus Christ.

128 Jesus freaks: The undesirables

The undesirables are the rejects from all parts of society. Like the lepers of Bible times, the undesirables have no one who loves them. They have been ostracized by friends, family, acquaintances—by everyone.

When no one loved us, Jesus loved us. When no one cared for us, Jesus cared for us. That is why we praise Him; that is why we worship Him. If people knew what we were going through, if people knew what we have already gone through, they would praise as we praise.

Jesus freaks: The unashamed

To understand the unashamed, we can take a look at Zacchaeus.

Then Jesus entered and walked through Jericho. There was a man there, his name Zacchaeus, the head tax man and quite rich. He wanted desperately to see Jesus, but the crowd was in his way—he was a short man and couldn't see over the crowd. So he ran on ahead and climbed up a sycamore tree so he could see Jesus when he came by.

When Jesus got to the tree, he looked up and said, "Zacchaeus, hurry down. Today is my day to be a guest in your home." Zacchaeus scrambled out of the tree, hardly believing his good luck, delighted to take Jesus home with him. Everyone who saw the incident was indignant and grumped, "What business does he have getting cozy with this crook?"

Zacchaeus just stood there, a little stunned. He stammered apologetically, "Master, I give away half my income to the poor—and if I'm caught cheating, I pay four times the damages."

Jesus said, "Today is salvation in this home! Here he is: Zacchaeus, son of Abraham! For the Son of Man came to find and restore the lost."

—Luke 19:1–10, *The Message*

129

Zacchaeus was short in stature, and needed to climb a tree in order to see Jesus. Like Zacchaeus, the Bible says that we are all "short":

For all have sinned and fall short of the glory of God.—Romans 3:23

In the third day, all short people need a tree. We have all sinned and fallen short of the glory of God. Two thousand years ago, God gave us a tree called Calvary so that we can climb and see His glory. Are there any tree climbers in this generation? Are you a tree climber?

✳ **Zacchaeus climbed a tree and saw Jesus. I climbed on the cross, and I have Jesus.**

✳ **The sycamore tree gives you a visitation; Calvary's tree gives you a habitation.**

God will never tell you, "Come down, because I am going to your house." He will tell you, "Come down, because you are coming to My house—I have a mansion waiting for you."

And if I go and prepare a place for you, I will come back again and receive you to Myself; that where I am, there you may be also.—JOHN 14:3

CLIMB THE TREE

God is not looking for tall people. He is looking for those who are short . . . those who have tried, but couldn't. He wants those who reached out but fell short . . . those who are not perfect. **He is not looking for giants—because He is the only giant in the land. He is looking for those who are willing to climb.** There is no way to see beyond the flesh . . . there is no other way to see beyond the world . . . there is no way to see beyond the fog in the midst of

130

If Zacchaeus could climb a tree and provoke Jesus to visit him, we can climb on the cross and provoke Jesus to live with us.

humanity, carnality and immorality. You need to climb on the cross. There is no way to see beyond yourself, unless you climb on the cross.

Third Day freaks not only climb the tree—but they climb the mountain to acquire the tree.

POSITION, PROMOTION, PRIESTHOOD

Third Day freaks climb up to acquire the tree. Third Day freaks understand that they must rise up with Third Day feet—the feet of position, promotion and priesthood. The devil does not belong in heaven or in the minds, hearts or families of God's people. He belongs underneath your feet—not the feet of sinners, but the feet of saints. The devil needs to know that there is a faithful remnant that will not bow down.

> *Then He said, "Do not draw near this place. Take your sandals off your feet, for the place where you stand is holy ground."*
> —EXODUS 3:5

Your feet must be holy. You must take off your sandals. Bare feet lead to a bare anointing. He does not want to touch your sandals; He wants to touch you. Priestly feet are holy; get the sin off your feet. Shake the dust off; shake off your humanity.

131

> *Shake yourself from the dust, arise; sit down, O Jerusalem! Loose yourself from the bonds of your neck, O captive daughter of Zion!*—ISAIAH 52:2

The Bible tells us that if we are rejected, we need to shake the dust off and leave that place (Matt. 10:14).

Shake the dust off in the name of Jesus. Walk after the Spirit, as we read in Romans 8:1:

> *There is therefore now no condemnation to those who are in Christ Jesus, who do not walk according to the flesh, but according to the Spirit.*

We need to rise up with Third Day feet. We are not first day Pharisees or second day followers. We are Third Day freaks.

ANOINTED TO CRUSH

Why did Mary anoint the feet of Jesus? She did it to get them ready to crush the devil's head. The Lamb of God crushed the serpent's head. You are about to get ready to crush, because the anointing crushes the yoke. Step on it, and crush it according to Luke 10:19:

> *Behold, I give you the authority to trample on serpents and scorpions, and over all the power of the enemy, and nothing shall by any means hurt you.*

Crush the yoke of bondage in the name of Jesus. Crush those circumstances around you. Make the circumstances around you a wine press. Crush the things around you that need to be crushed in order for vintage wine to flow forth.

132

God has given us two feet—one with which to possess, and one with which to crush. If we put them both together, we can dance and rejoice before the Lord. Crush the enemy by dancing before God.

DANCE BEFORE GOD

Christians should not be afraid to dance. I do not understand the second day concept of dancing as a Christian. In

Genesis we can see the Spirit hovering and dancing over the face of the waters. The psalmist declared, "You have turned for me my mourning into dancing" (Ps. 30:11). King David danced before the Lord with all his might. Miriam danced before the Lord in the Book of Exodus. Before the feast of the tabernacles, God's people danced because of His forgiveness.

> Friend, when you dance under the anointing of God . . . for the glory of God . . . in praise and worship unto God . . . the devil cannot touch you.

In a recent boxing title fight between Oscar De La Hoya and Felix Tito Trinidad, a very powerful truth was brought home to me. Oscar had a very unique strategy. At the end of the fight, the ring announcer asked him, "Why did you change your strategy? What was so different—all you did was dance?" Oscar's response was powerful. He said, "The more I danced around the ring, the more Tito was frustrated with me. Besides that, when I dance around, the enemy cannot touch me."

The discos, the clubs and the arenas should not be filled with the greatest of dancers. The greatest of dancers are those who come and rejoice before the presence of God. We do not need to secularize or allow worldly influences to permeate our beings and our church. Dance is not an origination of the enemy—it is an origination of the kingdom of God. It is an instrument of praise and worship. Third Day worshipers will not be afraid to rejoice and dance before the holy of holies.

If God can stand up, spin and dance over me, how much more should I stand up, dance and rejoice before Him for all He has done? Should we make dance a theological foundation? Absolutely not! Should dance be a doctrine?

133

Absolutely not—it is a method, a different way to praise and worship.

CULTURE SHOCK

Cultures around the world celebrate victories by dancing. We must be careful not to create a Christianity based upon a particular culture. By *culture* I mean an ethnic group, a race or a specific denomination. There are cultures that do things that, in our culture, we may find intolerable or unacceptable. As long as they do not violate Scripture, it is within the cultural freedom of each particular group of people to praise and worship the Lord as that culture sees fit. We should not be first day Pharisees, condemning or criticizing, or second day followers, going along with every flow.

We must be Third Day freaks, leading the way to a great revival . . . rising up in praise and worship in celebration and anointing. But above all things, we must do it according to God's Word and in God's holy truth.

THIRD DAY FEET

Priestly feet are anointed to possess. We have been using our feet to run away when we should be using them to possess.

> *Every place that the sole of your foot will tread upon I have given you, as I said to Moses.*—Joshua 1:3

It is time for you to take hold of your marriage, your home and your neighborhood. It is your time to put on *Jehovah-nissi* and present the banner of God.

*** It is time for possession where you are.**

* It is time for ownership.

* It is time for promotion—you're not bronze, you are gold.

* It is time to stop renting and start owning, to stop borrowing and start lending.

* This is the time to go from being employed to being an employer, from laborer to manager.

* It is time to go from being a follower to a leader, from a victim to a conqueror.

It is *your* time, for you are a Third Day Jesus freak.

RELEASED IN THE THIRD DAY

Jonah was released from the belly of the whale on the third day. Let this be the day when the body of Christ becomes intolerable to the world.

Jesus Christ will return for us when the world casts us out. Jesus Christ will have no other choice but to pick us up.

Let the Third Day worshipers be released by the world because it cannot swallow us any longer.

When the world says, "We cannot have you here any longer because your holiness and integrity are so powerful . . . the glory of God is so strong in your life that we cannot tolerate you any longer," let them cast us out. Let us become the rejects and the undesirables again.

135

Jesus didn't hang around those who were accepted and popular . . . those who were the epitome of success and fame. He hung around those who were rejected. He ministered to the disenfranchised, the hurting. **He walked and talked and breathed and preached with the undesirables, the rejects, the upsetters and the unashamed. He met with lonely people.** Third Day worshipers will be found alone at times.

If you are a Third Day worshiper, you may be rejected by those in your inner circle—as well as by the world. You will pray differently, praise differently and worship differently. They may believe what you believe—but you will live it out differently because not only do you believe it in your heart, you believe it in your head and in your hands. You

I want an anointing that makes the devils and demons shake and tremble when they see me because the glory of God is upon me.

believe it internally and externally. You believe it in your actions, in your reason, in your intellect and in your spirit. You execute and act according to it. In this way, Third Day worshipers are different from first and second day worshipers. For this reason, we are known as Jesus freaks.

We are the upsetters, the unashamed, the undesirables and the rejected. A Third Day worshiper must become accustomed to the cave and to the Garden of Gethsemane. The Third Day worshiper will remain when everyone else has left after a great outpouring. When God asks, "What are you doing here?" you will reply, "Waiting for more." A Third Day worshiper is the first one to arrive and the last one to leave. A Third Day worshiper wants more of Him—not what He has to give, but who He is.

REVIVAL THROUGHOUT THE LAND

We praise God for all the revivals and outpourings of His

136

Spirit that are occurring across America and around the world. Praise the Lord for Pensacola and Smithton. Praise the Lord for New York, California and Washington. Praise the Lord for revivals in Argentina, Brazil, Korea, the Philippines, Ukraine, Africa, India and the Czech Republic.

But I challenge you to go further than revival. Third Day Jesus freaks must understand that revival is only the first step. God wants to raise us up after He revives us so that we may live in His sight.

We must change the paradigm of the body of Christ in the third day. We will go beyond revival. The anointing of the Third Day Jesus freak does not merely slay the saint in the Holy Spirit—it slays the devils and demons around you. I want an anointing that goes beyond me falling on the ground. I want an anointing that hurls the demons and devils around me to the ground. I want an anointing that goes beyond making me twitch, jerk and shutter.

> We move the devil with our praise, and we move God with our worship.

Friend, under the anointing of God, we can expect the supernatural at all times—unrestricted, unlimited, unhampered and forever more.

AN ANOINTING TO DIE FOR

With the Third Day anointing, we pray differently. We pray prophetically. We pray through Scripture. We pray believing everything that God has promised us. **We pray with expectation. We pray in the Spirit. We pray with a language that is not our own. We pray without ceasing.**

We are fanatical; our praise is loud and violent, and our worship reaches the heart of God. The gates of hell are

137

shut tight and every enemy is bound up and cast out when we praise.

THE FOOLS
THAT WON THE PRIZE

I am a fool—the greatest of fools. I am a fool for Him. One day the newspaper headlines will declare . . .

* "Rejects Become Rulers"
* "Freaks Become Kings"
* "Sinners Are Now Saints"
* "Warriors Are Today's Greatest Worshipers"

It is important to understand that Jesus did not come down to earth just so He could become human like us. More importantly, He came down to earth so that we can become like Him.

One day the Emergency Broadcast System is going to announce a legitimate, powerful emergency—one that all the networks and TV stations throughout the world will report. Their report will be something like this:

A few minutes ago we confirmed information from the United Nations that in every nation across the world the same thing is happening. Ladies and gentlemen, we are declaring worldwide martial law as a result of this great catastrophe, which, our NASA director reports, happened in the twinkling of an eye.

It appears that those people who lifted up their hands to worship God in Spirit and in truth . . . those who declared themselves to be born again . . . those who declared power in the blood of Jesus . . . those who said their sins had been washed away by the blood of the Lamb . . . those who believed the Bible was infallible truth . . . those Jesus freaks have disappeared. They are no longer here. They no longer abide upon this planet. The freaks are gone.

138

That is the destiny of a Third Day worshiper, the destiny of the Third Day Jesus freak.

THE VOICE

So I speak to you who have sometimes felt rejected, you who have considered yourself on more than one occasion to be a legitimate undesirable. You who have upset many with your praise and worship, your zeal and holiness, your perseverance and passion. You are a Third Day Jesus freak. You are a Third Day worshiper. Your destiny is secured; your future is guaranteed. Everything God promised you, friend, in the third day it will come to pass.

"Father . . . "

"Yes, My Son, what is it?"

"We found them."

"You found whom, My Son?"

"Those for whom I have been searching since the beginning of creation. Our search is over, Father. We have been searching for those who would worship in Spirit and truth. In this third day, the search is over. We found them on their knees, on their face, prostrate with their hands stretched out. Father, look at the tear rolling down the cheek of that young man. That tear is more powerful than any other song heard in the heavens or played by multitudes of angels. That single teardrop resonates with the music of grace and divine perfection. That shout within that young man, that former addict, is not just any shout. That shout does not come from the vocal cord of that believer; it comes from the belly of a changed life.

"That hand being lifted up by that woman, Father, is no longer lifted in defense against abuse, but in proclamation of victory. There she is with her hands lifted up in surrender unto Me.

"Father, look at the quiet one. She does nothing but smile. No noise, no words, no expression. Nevertheless, from her flows a river

139

like a clear, crystal stream. The silence of the believer is greater than the shout of a sinner.

"We found them, Father, the fools, the freaks, the unashamed, the upsetters, the undesirables and the rejects. We found the true worshipers who worship Me in Spirit and in truth. The search is over. Sound the alarm."

Are you Third Day?

Raise Us Up to Breakthrough in Bethany

Flabbergasted, *bewildered*, **indignant.** I cried out, "How could He? How could He? How could He? How could Christ permit Lazarus to die? I do not understand. He received the news, yet He waited. He waited for Lazarus to die. How could He?"

In the third day, we look beyond declarations that are confessional. We look beyond the positive inclinations of our minds.

* **No matter how much positive confession is done . . .**

* **No matter how many hankies are sent out through the mail . . .**

* **No matter how many times hands are placed on the television screen . . .**

* **No matter how many times things are repeated time and time again . . .**

Lazarus, nevertheless, died. Why did God permit Lazarus to die? In the third day, we receive revelation and illumination regarding the Word.

God doesn't reside in
mansions and palaces;
He is not limited to
pulpits or crusades.
He enters our lives.

I understand there are times when God does permit us to die. I understand there are things that we want God to fix and heal, but He would rather have them dead and buried. He is waiting for those things to pass away in order to call us out and release us unto full glorification of Himself in us, His body.

Yes, friend, there are times when God will permit you to die.

* He permits you to die, to resurrect you to a greater state than before.

* He permits you to die, to raise you up to be better than yesterday.

* He permits you to die, to send you out to higher places than you could ever imagine.

GET READY TO REJOICE

Christ enters Bethany, the city of woes.

Christ resides

* wherever there is a broken heart,
* wherever there is a vast void,
* wherever there is a shed tear,
* wherever there is an anguished soul,
* wherever there is a hurt spirit.

142

Christ is there. He is within the city of woes. Jesus always returns to Bethany. Praise is about to break out in Bethany. A shout is about to break out in Bethany. A dance is about to break out in Bethany.

✴ **Get ready to praise.**
✴ **Get ready to shout.**
✴ **Get ready to dance.**
✴ **Get ready to worship.**
✴ **Get ready to rejoice.**

The Master is coming.

When Jesus heard that, He said, "This sickness is not unto death, but for the glory of God, that the Son of God may be glorified through it."—JOHN 11:4

Your sickness is not for death. It is for God to be glorified. You are the motive, my friend. You are the reason God is coming to Bethany. You are the reason the Master is returning to this planet of woes. That sickness, that burden, that struggle, that yoke you carry right now will allow God to be glorified in you.

In the midst of a troubled world, in the midst of chaos and anarchy, there is hope that at any moment the Master is coming.

It is a temporary thing. It will pass away, not because you convinced your mind that it will, but because the Bible says it. God will be glorified. Because Jesus loves you, He will do it. Jesus loved Lazarus.

143

Now Jesus loved Martha and her sister and Lazarus.—JOHN 11:5

WE MUST DIE TO LIVE

Jesus loved. Therefore stop asking God to heal those things that He is trying to kill. Let them die.

* **Let sin die.**
* **Let the flesh die.**
* **Let your ambitions die.**
* **Let your objectives die.**
* **Let your disposition die.**
* **Let your presumptions die.**
* **Let your prejudices die.**
* **Let your biases die.**
* **Let your limitations die.**

Let Jesus live!

There are certain things that need to die in order for Christ to release you.

Some things have to die before He releases you, before He calls you and sends you out. Lazarus had to die before Christ could release him out of the grave and send him out as a witness of God's enormous power.

So, when He heard that he was sick, He stayed two more days in the place where He was.—JOHN 11:6

Jesus waited until Lazarus died—for in his death the glory of God could be seen. In the Old Covenant, the glory of God was the manifest presence of God. Not only did it bring security to the people of Israel, but simultaneously the glory of God could bring death. If it was handled inappropriately, it brought about death. When placed in a place it did not belong, it brought about death.

So they set the ark of God on a new cart, and brought it out of the house of Abinadab . . . and Uzzah and Ahio, the sons of

144

> *Abinadab, drove the new cart . . . Then
> David and all the house of Israel played
> music before the LORD . . . And when they
> came to Nachon's threshing floor, Uzzah
> put out his hand to the ark of God and took
> hold of it, for the oxen stumbled. Then the
> anger of the LORD was aroused against
> Uzzah, and God struck him there for his
> error; and he died there by the ark of God.*
> —2 SAMUEL 6:3–7

The glory of God is a dichotomous glory—it not only brings life, but it also brings death.

God is waiting for you to die so that He can visit you, abide in you and make you live.

When the glory visits you, my friend, your spirit comes to life, and your flesh dies. The inner man comes to life, and the outer man dies.

Two days after Lazarus died, Jesus prepared to go to Judea to the home of Mary and Martha in Bethany. His disciples pleaded with him not to go.

> *Then after this He said to the disciples,
> "Let us go to Judea again." The disciples
> said to Him, "Rabbi, lately the Jews sought
> to stone You, and are You going there
> again?"—JOHN 11:7–8*

145

The devil didn't want Jesus to be glorified through Lazarus in Judea. The disciples told Jesus. "The last time You were there, they persecuted You. They attempted to stone You and to kill You." There are places the devil does not want you to go. There are people who will tell you not to go, not to execute your calling, not to do what God has told you to do.

People surrounding you—religious people and some second day people—do not want you to enter into your greatest day . . . your third day.

* **They will not articulate it in that manner.**

* **They will spiritualize it.**

* **They may even speak tongues upon you for confirmation.**

* **They may use their gift or their anointing to hinder you and hold you back.**

But in reality, when God calls you into Bethany, nothing can stop you. God is calling you to

* **the holy place,**
* **the throne of God,**
* **the hiding place,**
* **the prayer closet,**
* **the study of the Word.**

But you need to say, "I am going in!" Repeat after me right now: **"I'm going in; I'm going in.** Even though I may be bruised, I am going in. Even though I may be weary, I am going in. Even though I may be lonely, I am going in. Even though I may be brokenhearted, I am going in. **Even though I may be forgotten, I am going in. Even though I may be alienated, I am going in. Even though I may be pressed, I am going in. Even though I am dead, I am going in. I am going in!**

* **"I am going in with praise.**
* **"I am going in with worship.**

146

✳ "I am going in with rejoicing.
✳ "I am going in with celebration."

There are no walls the enemy can erect to keep us out. We have the anointing to knock those walls down in Jesus' name.

> *So the people shouted when the priests blew the trumpets. And it happened when the people heard the sound of the trumpet, and the people shouted with a great shout, that the wall fell down flat. Then the people went up into the city, every man straight before him, and they took the city.*—JOSHUA 6:20

Even though mountains stand in our path, I am going in. We will move them or climb them according to God's will.

> *So Jesus said to them, "Because of your unbelief; for assuredly, I say to you, if you have faith as a mustard seed, you will say to this mountain, 'Move from here to there,' and it will move; and nothing will be impossible for you."*—MATTHEW 17:20

Even if the fire of hell opposes me, I am going in.

> *When you pass through the waters, I will be with you; and through the rivers, they shall not overflow you. When you walk through the fire, you shall not be burned, nor shall the flame scorch you.*—ISAIAH 43:2

147

There are times we are confronted with such great truth that our initial reaction may be shock or denial. However, in the third day, we will receive this truth as fuel, not to

ARE YOU A THIRD DAY CHRISTIAN?

turn back or stop, but rather to go forward and go on to what God has promised us. It is during these times that our character is tested and tried in order to bear fruit that only Third Day determination can produce. Despite the circumstances, situations and conditions, even if I am the only one standing at the end of the road, I am going in—*and no one or nothing will stop me!*

THREE THIRD DAY WORSHIPERS

When Jesus arrived in Bethany, He encountered the reactions of both Mary and Martha:

> *Then Martha, as soon as she heard that Jesus was coming, went and met Him, but Mary was sitting in the house.*—John 11:20

Mary, Martha and Lazarus represent three types of Third Day characters that we will encounter.

Martha ran out to meet Jesus for her encounter with Him. Mary stayed in the house, waiting for her encounter. Mary had the inclination to wait as a worshiper. This same Mary anointed the feet of Jesus, pouring out expensive perfume and oil upon the feet of the Master. Why did Mary wait? Many have criticized Mary for waiting, intimating that a Martha spirit of constantly working may claim God's blessings faster. But I contend that in the third day we need to have a Mary spirit.

Martha ran; Mary waited; and Lazarus was released.

Martha came, not as a form of worship, but to criticize Jesus for permitting her brother to die. Mary waited because she knew that being at her Master's feet superseded any situation or circumstance.

She knew that when the Master arrived, everything would be all right.

148

Jesus said to her, "Your brother will rise again."—JOHN 11:23

Jesus declared, "Your brother shall live." On this third day, you need to declare that your brother shall live.

* **Your sister shall live.**
* **Your family shall live.**
* **Your finances shall live.**
* **Your marriage shall live.**
* **Your anointing shall live.**
* **Your ministry shall live.**
* **Your calling shall live.**

Right now, speak out, right where you are, that "my calling, my ministry, my future and my destiny shall live. **I am going to live, for I refuse to do anything else but live.**

* **"I refuse to be part of a dying world when I am part of a living church.**

* **"I refuse to be part of a dying destiny when I am part of a living legacy.**

* **"I am going to live. Right after I die, I am going to live."**

Jesus said to her, "I am the resurrection and the life. He who believes in Me, though he may die, he shall live."—JOHN 11:25

149

Friend, the more we die, the more we will live. When we fully die to ourselves, then and only then does the living Christ revive us and raise us up to live in His sight. We die in order to live. When we are truly dead to ourselves, we no longer are distracted by our own limitations. At that point, we do not see things our way nor do we hear things our way. We begin to hear the voice of God calling out to us. And despite our surroundings, faith is birthed, because the Teacher is calling for us.

> *And when she had said these things, she went her way and secretly called Mary her sister, saying, "The Teacher has come and is calling for you."—JOHN 11:28*

The Master has come, and He is calling for you. He is calling for whom? He is calling for Mary. Jesus waited for Mary before He continued. In other words, Jesus, who was close to the tomb, halfway there, was saying to Mary, "I will not do anything further until I have a real worshiper come before Me." He was waiting for a Third Day worshiper. He was waiting for a worshiper who worshiped Him in Spirit and in truth. Until that worshiper arrived, Jesus refused to go any further.

God is waiting for true worshipers to arrive. He is waiting for a Mary to meet Him halfway.

God will not release the anointing or call you out of your grave unless your true worship meets Him halfway.

✳ **Worship ignites the heart of God to perform the miracles.**

✳ **Worship provokes the glory of God to exercise the supernatural.**

He waited for Mary before He continued. He waits for a worshiper before He continues to move.

> *Then, when Mary came where Jesus was, and saw Him, she fell down at His feet, saying to Him, "Lord, if You had been here, my brother would not have died."—JOHN 11:32*

Once you have been at the Master's feet, your life will never be the same again.

Mary fell at His feet—where she had sat as He taught on an earlier occasion. The feet that shortly she would anoint in preparation for His sacrificial death.

There is something about being at the feet of Jesus. It is time to go to the feet of the Master.

* **In the first day we merely held on to His hands.**

* **In the second day we touched only the hem of His garment.**

* **But in the third day we embrace, anoint and kiss His feet.**

Christ's feet are the platform of forgiveness, power and grace. His feet possess power. We must hold on to the Master's feet. For it is His feet that crush the head of the enemy. His feet have the power to break the strongholds of the devil.

SEVEN STEPS TO RAISING UP

And He said, "Where have you laid him?" They said to Him, "Lord, come and see."
—*John 11:34*

There are seven steps that we all must take in order to come out of the grave.

151

* **Seven steps for raising things that are dead in our lives**

* **Seven steps for resurrecting and calling out**

You must identify the location of that ministry, that

anointing, that calling, that person. Identify the specific place. Where did you put that hurt you hid so deeply in your heart? Identify the specific chamber.

✳ **Where were you injured?**
✳ **Where were you victimized?**
✳ **Where were you abused?**

Go back to that place. It goes beyond some inner victimization type of New Age psychotherapeutic mumbo-jumbo where you try to bring out your inner child and acknowledge all the painful experiences in your past.

It is time for you to sit upon the things that at one time were holding you back.

There are some things better left buried. But there are some things God wants to resurrect. Those are the things that you should identify. Go back to the place with the anointing of the Holy Spirit. Then take each step to ultimate victory.

1 *Remove the rock*

Jesus said, "Take away the stone." Martha, the sister of him who was dead, said to Him, "Lord, by this time there is a stench, for he has been dead four days."—JOHN 11:39

152 Remove the thing that is impeding you, my friend. That which is impeding you from seeing your miracle must be removed.

On the day of Christ's resurrection, the women found the stone rolled away and an angel sitting upon the rock. Catch that picture—the angel *sat* upon the rock.

Sitting indicates that you rule! That rock that held you in your bondage has become your throne room.

✳ **You need to rule over your circumstances.**
✳ **You need to rule over your situations.**
✳ **You need to rule over your weakness.**

That temptation . . . vise . . . limitation . . . shortcoming . . . that at one time blocked you in is now the throne upon which you reign.

Now you sit on that rock. You rule over it, not for a day . . . not for a season . . . but forevermore. You sit upon that situation, **but God sits on you.** And as long as God sits on you, you

First day Pharisees throw stones; second day followers follow the stones; and Third Day freaks live on the stone.

will not be able to get out from that situation. You sit on it, meaning that you are ruling over it. **You are reigning over it.** If you move it, it might come back to haunt you. But if you sit upon it, you know exactly where it is. In the third day, we rule over our circumstances. **We are Third Day kings, and Third Day kings rule.**

2 *Believe*

> *Jesus said to her, "Did I not say to you that if you would believe you would see the glory of God?"—JOHN 11:40*

Believe, and you shall see the glory.

Believe and see, not see and believe. You are not a Thomas—you are a Third Day worshiper. You will believe it first, then you will see it. We believe it, and we receive it by faith.

> *Now faith is the substance of things hoped for, the evidence of things not seen. For by it the elders obtained a good testimony. By*

153

faith, we understand that the worlds were framed by the word of God, so that the things which are seen were not made of things which are visible.—HEBREWS 11:1–3

When you have faith, all things are possible through Christ Jesus. We are spiritual beings with human experiences; therefore we should continually operate by faith.

3 - 4 *Praise and worship*

Father, I thank You that You have heard Me. And I know that You always hear Me.
—JOHN 11:41–42

Jesus entered that situation of death with praise. He had a worship service before anything else.

God has already blessed you, friend. He blessed you two thousand years ago. But you are just now coming into the realization of that blessing. **He has already forgiven you for sins you have not yet committed. He has already healed you of diseases you have not yet had. He has already blessed you for things you have not yet asked Him for. He has already taken you out of circumstances you have not yet gone through. God is the same yesterday, today and forever. Everything He did, He did at the cross.** You are just now coming into the full acknowledgment of what He already did two thousand years ago.

We need to enter each situation we face with thanksgiving, declaring things already done.

We must come with prophetic thanksgiving. Stop praying, "Lord, save my son." Start thanking God for his salvation. Thank Him for the salvation of your daughter, your husband, your

154

marriage, your young people and your neighborhoods. Pray prophetically, praise prophetically, worship prophetically—think prophetically.

5 *Publicly acknowledge*

The cross was a public thing. Calvary is a public expression. Your Christianity must be a public expression.

> *Now when He had said these things, He cried with a loud voice, "Lazarus, come forth!"—JOHN 11:43*

The world needs our public acknowledgment of the glory of God upon our lives. Christ made sure everyone saw—and heard—of His Father's glory in the raising of Lazarus. The Third Day worshiper uses a shout, a noise, a loud voice to acknowledge the supernatural workings of God in his or her life.

6 *Come out; get it out*

> *And he who had died came out bound hand and foot with graveclothes, and his face was wrapped with a cloth.—JOHN 11:44*

Lazarus came out of his tomb with the exterior trappings of death still clinging to him. He was not content to stay in that tomb. He didn't even take the time to shed the trappings of death before he came out. Those graveclothes were designed to contain death—they could not contain resurrected life. The graveclothes . . . bondages . . . chains . . . situations and circumstances that contain you in death cannot hold you in resurrected life. Come out, come out, come out. Leave death behind, and enter life.

155

7 *Loosen it, and let it go*

> *Jesus said to them, "Loose him, and let him go."—JOHN 11:44*

It is not good enough for God just to call you out. Jesus called out Lazarus. But Jesus Himself did not loosen the graveclothes that bound him. He didn't get involved in the loosening process. No; you must meet God halfway. God will declare you. He will release you, but you are going to need some help in getting loosened from those bondages.

Surround yourself with people who are willing to loosen you when God calls you out. Surround yourself with Third Day believers who are willing to loosen your graveclothes to let you emerge in resurrection life.

Are you Third Day?

Raised Up As Third Day Mountain Climbers

Climb, *climb*, **climb**. Every time a man or woman has an encounter with a mountaintop, something supernatural happens.

> *"Go up to the mountains and bring wood and build the temple, that I may take pleasure in it and be glorified," says the* LORD. —HAGGAI 1:8

Third Day mountain climbers must climb the following mountains:

* Mount Ararat
* Mount Moriah
* Mount Olive
* Mount Carmel
* Mount Sinai
* The Mount of Transfiguration
* Mount Calvary
* Mount Zion

"Give me that mountain," Caleb cried out.

One day some men from the tribe of Judah went to Joshua at Gilgal. Among them was Caleb son of Jephunneh the Kenizzite. He

*said to Joshua, "You remember what the L*ORD *said at Kadesh
Barnea when he was speaking to the prophet Moses about you and
me. Moses, the L*ORD's *servant, sent me to look at the land where we
were going. I was forty years old then. When I came back, I told
Moses what I thought about the land. The other men who went with
me tried to frighten the people, but I fully believed the L*ORD *would
allow us to take the land. So that day Moses promised me, 'The land
where you went will become your land, and your children will own it
forever. I will give you that land because you fully believed in the
L*ORD, *my God.'*

*"Now then, the L*ORD *has kept his promise. He has kept me alive
for forty-five years from the time he said this to Moses during the
time we all wandered in the desert. Now I am eighty-five years old.
I am still as strong today as I was the day Moses sent me out, and I
am just as ready to fight now as I was then. So give me the mountain country the Lord promised me that day long ago. Back then
you heard that the Anakite people lived there and the cities were
large and well protected. But now with the L*ORD *helping me, I will
force them out, just as the L*ORD *said."*

*Joshua blessed Caleb son of Jephunneh and gave him the city of
Hebron as his own.*

—JOSHUA *14:6–13,* NCV

THIRD DAY MOUNTAIN CLIMBERS

158

Are there any Third Day mountain climbers who will
dare to stop crawling down in the foothills? God has not
called you to crawl; He has called you to climb the
mountain. The fastest way up the mountain is to run up
the mountain.

When Christ performed miracles, He made a declaratory
statement immediately after the miracle:

❋ "Arise, take up your bed, and go to your house."—*Luke 5:24*

❋ "Rise, take up your bed and walk."—*John 5:8*

❋ "Arise and stand here."—*Luke 6:8*

❋ "Arise, and do not be afraid."—*Matthew 17:7*

It is time for us to stand up and climb. God has not called us to crawl. Arise, and begin to climb.

❋ Stop crawling in your misery.
❋ Stop crawling in your failure.
❋ Stop crawling in your despair.
❋ Stop crawling in your yesterday.

It's time for you to climb! We climb from glory to glory, from mountaintop to mountaintop!

The Third Day experience is the difference between mountains and valleys. We cannot deny that valleys are necessary. In order to get from one mountaintop to another, one must go through a valley. A valley is the space between two mountains.

God is calling you to a fresh start, a renewal process.

You are tested in the valley, but you are blessed on the mountaintop. You are broken in the valley, but you are restored on the mountaintop.

There are several specific mountains that we must climb.

Mount Ararat

The first mountain that the Third Day mountain climber must climb is Mount Ararat. When the flood was over, God revealed Mount Ararat to Noah.

Then the ark rested in the seventh month,

159

the seventeenth day of the month, on the mountains of Ararat.—GENESIS 8:4

Mount Ararat is the mountain of renewal. Mount Ararat is the mountain of a fresh start. God is calling you to the top of Mount Ararat.

As Noah sensed that the great flood was nearly over and the waters began to recede, he sent a raven and a dove out of the ark to search for dry ground. (See Genesis 8:6–12.) The raven did not return to the ark. A raven will never bring back news—anything that is in darkness cannot bring back good news. But the dove returned with a freshly plucked olive leaf. A dove will always bring back good news—when the Spirit of God is our Comforter and Counselor, He will always bring back good news.

When your storm is over, you will be on top.

As a sign of God's covenant with man, God caused a rainbow to appear to Noah on that mountaintop. That rainbow was the color of grace—a sign that the rainstorm was over. And when that storm was over, Noah's ark didn't rest at the bottom of the mountain . . . it wasn't located halfway up the mountain . . . it rested on top of Mount Ararat.

I speak to you now, my friends. You who are in the midst of the storm . . . you who are in the midst of a flood . . . a Dove is approaching you right now with good news. The Spirit of God is about to tell you there is a rainbow shining across the horizon. When the storm is over, you will be on top.

Mount Sinai

Another mountain for Third Day mountain climbers to ascend is Mount Sinai.

160

In the third month after the children of Israel had gone out of the land of Egypt, on the same day, they came to the Wilderness of Sinai . . . And Moses went up to God, and the LORD called to him from the mountain, saying, . . . "You have seen what I did to the Egyptians, and how I bore you on eagles' wings and brought you to Myself. Now therefore, if you will indeed obey My voice and keep My covenant, then you shall be a special treasure to Me above all people; for all the earth is Mine. And you shall be to Me a kingdom of priests and a holy nation." . . .

Then the LORD said to Moses, "Go to the people and consecrate them today and tomorrow, and let them wash their clothes. And let them be ready for the third day. For on the third day the Lord will come down upon Mount Sinai in the sight of all the people." . . .

Then it came to pass on the third day, in the morning, that there were thunderings and lightnings, and a thick cloud on the mountain; and the sound of the trumpet was very loud, so that all the people who were in the camp trembled. And Moses brought the people out of the camp to meet with God, and they stood at the foot of the mountain. Now Mount Sinai was completely in smoke, because the LORD descended upon it in fire . . . and the whole mountain quaked greatly. And when the blast of the trumpet sounded long and became louder and louder, Moses spoke, and God answered him by voice. Then the LORD came down upon Mount Sinai, on the top of the mountain. And the LORD called Moses to the top of the mountain, and Moses went up. . . .

161

Now the glory of the LORD rested on Mount Sinai, and the cloud covered it six days. And on the seventh day He called to Moses out of the midst of the cloud. The sight of the glory of the LORD was like a consuming fire on the top of the mountain in the eyes of the children of Israel.

—EXODUS *19:1, 3–6, 10–11, 16–20; 24:16–17*

ARE YOU A THIRD DAY CHRISTIAN?

The glory of God rested on Mount Sinai. The tablets of
stone containing the Ten Commandments were placed
in the hands of Moses on Mount Sinai. Mount Sinai is
the mountain of impartation where God will impart His
law . . . His Word . . . His blessing upon your life.

> ✳ **It is the mountain where your face will
> change.**

> ✳ **It is the mountain where your posture will
> change.**

> ✳ **It is the mountain where your anointing and
> your ministry will change.**

God is about to take you to Mount Sinai. God is about
to place something in your hands. At this very moment,
the glory and the Word are being placed in your hands
upon Mount Sinai.

Mount Carmel

Mount Carmel is the mountain of confrontation . . . the
mountain of fire . . . the mountain of rain. It is the
mountain where the prophets surround you.

> *"Now therefore, send and gather all Israel to
> me on Mount Carmel, the four hundred
> and fifty prophets of Baal, and the four hun-
> dred prophets of Asherah, who eat at
> Jezebel's table." So Ahab sent for all the
> children of Israel, and gathered the prophets
> together on Mount Carmel.*—1 Kings 18:19–20

When you climb Mount Carmel as a Third Day mountain climber, the fire of the Holy Spirit in you will
quench the false prophets around you.

Mount Carmel represents the destruction of false

162

prophets. On it the Third Day altar was created, representing the reality that God is a God of fire. On that same mountaintop a weather report will be given calling for rain. Because a group of Third Day worshipers will be willing to climb, a small cloud will appear over them, pouring out significant rain. That rain will contain

✳ **greatest Third Day blessings,**

✳ **a great Third Day revival, raising us up to live in God's sight,**

✳ **a great Third Day renewal,**

✳ **the greatest empowerment of God's glory of all time.**

The Mount of Transfiguration

The Mount of Transfiguration is the mountain of change.

> *Now after six days Jesus took Peter, James, and John his brother, led them up on a high mountain by themselves; and He was transfigured before them. His face shone like the sun, and His clothes became as white as the light.—MATTHEW 17:1–2*

Jesus is the One who changes water into wine . . . tax collectors into soulwinners . . . and sinners into saints. The Mount of Transfiguration is the mountain of change. God changes the old things into new things:

163

> *Therefore, if anyone is in Christ, he is a new creation; the old has gone, the new has come!—2 CORINTHIANS 5:17, NIV*

The Third Day church is an agile church—able to deal with continuous change, progressing in an evolutionary process from glory to glory. In the midst of the change occurring on the Mount of Transfiguration, two prophets, Elijah and Moses, appeared with Christ. Why Elijah and Moses? And why did Christ appear in the midst of them?

There is one underlying characteristic that connects Elijah and Moses—they were both prophets of fire. In Moses' first encounter with God, God was in the form of a burning bush. God Himself followed Moses at night as a pillar of fire. Elijah called upon the Lord, and fire fell across the altars of the false prophets.

> God is always in the middle of people who are on fire.

God is a God of fire. God rests . . . God lives . . . God moves . . . and God inhabits people who are on fire. **God is always in the midst of people who are on fire. In order for God to change you, you need to be in the fire.** The fire is necessary for change.

My friend, sometimes it is not the devil that puts you in the fire—it is God.

> *Then Nebuchadnezzar went near the mouth of the burning fiery furnace and spoke, saying, "Shadrach, Meshach, and Abed-Nego, servants of the Most High God, come out, and come here." Then Shadrach, Meshach, and Abed-Nego came from the midst of the fire.*—DANIEL 3:26

164

These three young men entered the fiery furnace bound and chained, but when they walked out they were free from bondage. Why, that fire was not a satanic fire—*that fire was a holy fire.* The fourth man in the middle was Jesus! The God of fire in the middle made that fire a holy fire. Hallelujah!

You are not in the midst of a firestorm for Satan to annihilate you, but for God to elevate you to your next mountaintop, which is Mount Calvary.

In order for God to change you, you need to be in the fire. That is why you are going through what you are going through. That is why you are surrounded by the circumstances that surround you. You are not in the fire so the devil can destroy you—you are in the fire so God can change you.

Mount Calvary

All Third Day mountain climbers must climb Mount Calvary. It is that mountain where God converts that hill of garbage into a mountain of victory. God converts a hill to a mountain . . . a garbage heap to a victory celebration. Jesus died so that you can live. You must die to yourself so that He can live in you

> *I have been crucified with Christ; it is no longer I who live, but Christ lives in me; and the life, which I now live in the flesh I live by faith in the Son of God, who loved me and gave Himself for me.*—GALATIANS 2:20

It is time to ascend Mount Calvary—the mountain of redemption . . . the mountain of forgiveness . . . the mountain of grace.

165

Mount Zion

Third Day mountain climbers, get ready!

✶ **Third Day mountain climbers, be prepared.**
✶ **Third Day mountain climbers, pack your bags.**

The time has come to climb Mount Zion. Who shall ascend to God's holy mountain?

> *Who may ascend into the hill of the LORD? Or who may stand in His holy place? He who has clean hands and a pure heart, who has not lifted up his soul to an idol, nor sworn deceitfully. He shall receive blessing from the LORD, and righteousness from the God of his salvation.*—PSALM 24:3–5

This is our destiny, Third Day mountain climber. When you reach the top of this mountain, the King of glory steps in, seeking those who will live in His presence. After two days He will revive us; in the third day He will restore us that we may live in His presence.

Blow the trumpet in Zion . . . the mount where we sound the alarm . . . the mount where I am not only a survivor. I am an overcomer.

The finest wood is found in the highest of mountains.

> *"Go up to the mountains and bring wood and build the temple, that I may take pleasure in it and be glorified," says the* LORD.—HAGGAI 1:8

Upon Mount Calvary . . . upon Golgotha . . . upon the greatest mountain . . . is found the cross of Christ. The time has come to bring down the cross! Bring it down, and display it to all the people. Infiltrate the world with it.

What happens when we bring down the cross? We bring down divine interruption to the circumstances of the natural world. The things that "should not happen" do happen because of that divine interruption.

* Sarah was not supposed to get pregnant.

* The Red Sea was not supposed to part.

* The Jordan River was not supposed to part.

* The walls of Jericho were not supposed to fall.

* Jonah was not supposed to escape from the whale.

* The Hebrew boys were not supposed to live in the fire.

* Christ was not supposed to resurrect.

I have news for you! Sarah became pregnant . . . both the Jordan River and the Red Sea parted . . . the walls of Jericho fell . . . **Jonah was released from the whale . . .** the Hebrew boys were not burned in the **fire . . . and Christ has resurrected!**

You are not supposed to be alive right now. You should be somewhere in a hospital room . . . in the corner . . . in a prison cell . . . in an alley. You should be broken . . . destroyed . . . in pain . . . but you're not. Do you know why? Because God interrupted. When God came into the picture, there was a divine interruption. Someone brought the cross down and placed it into your heart.

> The cross does not belong in the mountain; it belongs in the hearts of people around this world.

This is the time to bring down the cross.

Without the cross we are powerless . . . without the cross we are going to hell. But with the cross the gates of hell shall not . . . will not . . . cannot prevail against you. With the cross . . .

✳ **You can do it.**
✳ **You have been forgiven.**
✳ **You have been delivered.**
✳ **You have been healed.**

Christ has done it all. Hell was not built for you—you can't fit into hell when you carry the cross. The cross does not symbolize defeat . . . it does not symbolize darkness. Although the reality of the cross was tragic, it is the best thing that has occurred since the beginning of time.

Jesus Christ was not defeated on the cross! The devil did not crucify Jesus—Jesus crucified Jesus. He became sin when sin He knew not.

> *For God so loved the world, that he gave his only begotten Son, that whosoever believeth in him should not perish, but have everlasting life.*—JOHN 3:16, KJV

You won at the cross. I won at the cross. The devil lost at the cross. Carry your cross. In the first and second days we thought that we were carrying a cross of victory. In the third day we understand that we carry

168

✳ **the instrument of the devil's defeat,**
✳ **the ultimate conquering of death,**
✳ **the powerful anointing of the Holy Spirit,**
✳ **the priceless gift of forgiveness,**
✳ **the foundation of our faith,**
✳ **the evidence of our redemption,**
✳ **the miracle of our healing.**

Bring down the cross . . . begin the revolution of the cross! The devil can break through metal, steel and iron, but he can't break through the old rugged cross. He can't break you.

The devil knocks you down, but the cross picks you up. You can cross over to eternity because of the cross. You can cross right out of hell and into heaven.

On the cross the *logos* Word became *rhema* flesh. Because of the cross, Jesus Christ was crucified a sacrifice, was resurrected a praise and is coming back as a worship.

The cross was not a private thing; it was a public thing. The cross is not to be carried privately; it is to be carried publicly.

* ✱ Vladimir Lenin said that by the year 2000, Communism would be the religion of the world.

* ✱ Hitler declared that the Third Reich would be greater than any Christian relief mentality.

* ✱ The Beatles declared that they were more popular than the Father, the Son and the Holy Spirit.

I have news for you. Lenin is dead, and Hitler is gone. The Beatles don't exist. But Jesus Christ is alive and well in the third day!

BRING IT DOWN

Without the presence of God you can't heal the sick. You can't move mountains, and you can't walk on water. Your hands are just hands, and your feet are just feet. The noise

169

that we make in churches is just noise, and the churches themselves are just buildings and auditoriums. But in the presence of Jesus, everything changes. With Jesus you can heal the sick in His name. You can move mountains. You can walk on water.

Your hands are not just hands; they are instruments of war. Your feet are not just feet; they are instruments of possession and crushing.

Bring down the presence of God. If the world can curse their way to hell, we can praise our way to heaven. We, the Third Day worshipers, are the most dangerous people in the world. In the third day, we do not need parishioners—we need worshipers . . . we don't need position seekers—we need presence seekers . . . we don't need worshipers in the temple—we need armies of worshipers.

Bring down the cross. Bring down the living God . . . the God who sings . . . the God who rejoices . . . the God who dances. Bring down the testimony of the Third Day mountain climber. Bring down the testimony in the midst of high schools and colleges. Teach our young people to bring down the testimony in the middle of a science class when the teacher begins to explain Darwin's evolutionary theory. In the second day many would be silent. Only the radical enough would say, "I do not believe in evolution."

Now in the third day they are going to take it one step further; Third Day Jesus freaks . . . Third Day worshipers . . . Third Day mountain climbers will assert, "We also believe in evolution."

When the teacher replies, "What do you mean that you also believe in evolution?", they will testify, "But not in your evolution. We do not believe that at one time we were amoebas that became paramecia . . . then tadpoles . . . then frogs . . . then lizards . . . then alligators . . . then chimpanzees . . . then *Homo erectus*—and here we are today.

"No, we believe in another kind of evolution. We believe that at one time we were sinners, but now we are saints. We believe in divine evolution. We were lost, but now we are found. We were blind, but now we see. We believe in divine change . . . in divine transformation—we believe in holy Third Day evolution!"

We believe that every sinner can become a saint when he experiences the redemptive power of Jesus Christ. Bring down the testimony in schools, homes, neighborhoods, colleges and churches. Bring down His glory; bring down His anointing.

STIR IT UP

After we bring it down, we stir it up. The same root word used in "stirring it up" is used in Haggai 1, John 5 and 2 Timothy 1:

> *So the* LORD *stirred up the spirit of Zerubbabel.*—HAGGAI 1:14, NIV

> *"Sir," the invalid replied, "I have no one to help me into the pool when the water is stirred."*—JOHN 5:7, NIV

> *Therefore I remind you to stir up the gift of God which is in you.*—2 TIMOTHY 1:6

What does "stirring it up" mean? It means taking things from the bottom and bringing them to the top. Friend, you and I used to be at the bottom, but God has called us to the top. God turned us around—He took us from the bottom of hell and brought us to the top of His glory.

171

Chefs use wooden spoons to preserve the integrity of the taste of the ingredients in their recipes. Two thousand years ago Jesus died on a wooden cross in order to pour His life into us and to stir up the greatness inside of us. It is not good enough to just put the spoon in the pot— you must stir up the ingredients . . . move things around. We move things around in our lives by rejoicing. When we move around with God, then God moves around the things in our lives that need to change. Things are stirred up . . . family members may be at the bottom of hell, but God can stir them up for heaven.

THE THIRD DAY SUPERNATURAL

I heard of a recent Third Day supernatural occurrence in Lubbock, Texas.

A woman who had attended our conference in Dallas, where I ministered on the third day, was involved in an automobile accident in Lubbock, Texas. Her child, who was riding in the car, was severely injured and lay in a coma in his hospital room. However, his mother remembered the words we had shared regarding rejoicing. She recalled the teaching about the sword of the Garden of Eden spinning around and our need to proclaim our blessings to the North, South, East and West. She knew that God rejoices over us, spins over us, and that we spin under Him.

As she sat in her son's hospital room, she began to rejoice. Even though the doctors had told her that her son might die, that even if he did live, he would no doubt remain in a vegetative state and be incapacitated for life, she rejoiced. On the third day of his hospital stay, the child awoke—completely healed, with no permanent injuries.

172

Rejoice; again I say, rejoice. Rejoice is synonymous with stirring it up.

SHAKE IT OUT

God is shaking the nation. He is shaking the Third Day mountain climber, the Third Day Jesus freak, **the Third Day worshiper. Indeed, He will shake the nations.** The arrival of Third Day Jesus freaks will shake the nations like never before. The nations are being shaken by the power of the glory of God. A Third Day worshiper is the glory of Christ Jesus.

> *The glory of this latter house shall be greater than of the former, saith the LORD of hosts: and in this place will I give peace, saith the LORD of hosts.* —HAGGAI 2:9, KJV

Christ is the glory of God; the church is the glory of Jesus.

We are to bring down the glory of God to our world. We are to stir it up and shake it out. We need to shake out His anointing . . . His victory . . . His truth. Shake out the Third Day message that Jesus Christ is Lord and there is no other but Him.

In the second day we were mountain movers; in the third day we are mountain climbers.

I speak to you, my friend. I speak to you, my fellow Third Day mountain climber. Climb up the mountain, bring down the cross, stir it up and shake it out. Climb that situation before you. You must make the choice to climb it to victory in this third day.

In the second day, all we did was move mountains. Some of those mountains were not intended to be moved—they were intended to be climbed.

On top of every mountain there is a blessing waiting for us.

173

God wants those who don't try to move circumstances out of their way. He want those who climb on top of them and reign.

More importantly, the Blesser awaits us on Mount Zion. Climb, climb. Exercise your knees; open up your lungs, for the air is thinner the higher you go. Your flesh will become weaker and weaker in the thinning, sacred air—but the presence of God will make you stronger spiritually.

Climb, climb, climb. Get your blessing. Bring it down. Stir up your family . . . neighborhood . . . church . . . community . . . ministry . . . anointing. Shake it out. Then climb again. We go from mountaintops to valley to mountaintop. No longer do we move the mountains—we climb them.

In the third day, God is not looking for mountain movers—He is looking for mountain climbers.

Don't just move your problem—rule over it. Declare victory over it. Are you a second day mountain mover or a Third Day mountain climber?

Are you Third Day?

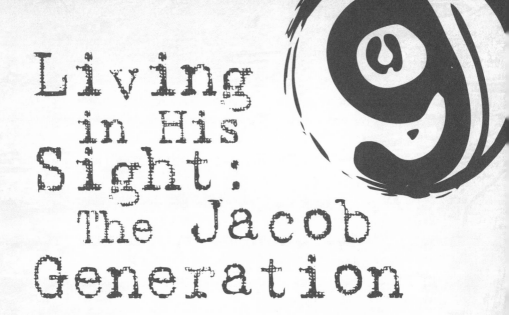

Living in His Sight: The Jacob Generation

Living in His sight; *living in His presence;* **living in His glory.** Imaginable to the human mind, desirable for the human spirit and destiny for the Third Day song. Living in His sight.

> *After two days He will revive us; on the third day He will raise us up, that we may live in His sight.*—Hosea 6:2

To live in His sight is to live in His presence—not merely *before* His presence, but *in it.*

✴ **As if somehow we would be able to enter in**

✴ **As if somehow truly the veil would be broken**

✴ **As if somehow we would lose our flesh, our shell, and be able to go inside of Him**

What an incredible perspective—living in His presence! Undeniably it is the yearning of our souls.

Second day Christians would visit, but Third Day Christians will live in His presence—every second of every minute . . . every minute of every hour . . . every hour of every day . . . throughout all eternity.

The Jacob generation will live in His presence. You may ask, "Why Jacob?" Because the Third Day generation is the generation of Jacob.

✳ **Abraham was the first generation of faith.**

✳ **Isaac was the second generation.**

✳ **The third generation of faith is the Jacob generation.**

The destiny of the Third Day worshiper is to live in God's presence.

Jacob means "deceiver." This generation is going to deceive again. The Third Day generation, the Jacobs of the third day who live in His sight, are going to deceive. Whom are we going to deceive? We are going to fool the enemy!

✳ **When the enemy thinks that he has knocked us down, we will rise up with a great anointing to destroy his every work and kingdom.**

✳ **When the devil thinks we are destroyed, we will get up.**

✳ **When the devil thinks it's over for us, that is when we are about to begin.**

176

✳ **When the devil thinks that we will never be able to succeed, we will conquer worlds and nations for Jesus!**

When the devil thinks that you will never be able to pray as you prayed before, you will say, "You are right. I am not going to pray as I prayed before. I am going to pray with and under a Third Day anointing . . . with a Third Day prophetic spirit . . . through the Word, with the

Word, by the Word." We will accomplish greater things in Jesus' name.

The enemy will be fooled by the Jacobs of the third day. When he thinks you are going out, you will be coming in. When he thinks you are coming in, you will be going out. The pillar of fire and the cloud were a confusion in the Book of Exodus. It was God's methodology of confusion against the enemy. When the enemy looked for them in darkness, the people of God were under the light. When the enemy looked at them in light, they were under the fire.

As a Third Day worshiper, you are part of the Jacob generation. You have been called for this hour to live in His sight.

Do you understand that? This means that the enemy could never find them, because he was at the wrong place at the wrong time. Understand that we are going to fool the enemy. It is our time to fool the enemy!

When the enemy thinks that we are going to be administering things, we are going to be in God's holy presence. When the enemy thinks that we are going to be building our own platforms, we are going to build a platform for God and get out of the way. When the enemy thinks that we are going to descend, we are actually going to be descending to pick up his keys in order to annihilate his kingdom. Yell out with me . . .

✳ "It's not over until I win!
✳ "It's not over until I have the final victory!
✳ "It's not over until I have the final battle!"

The enemy has knocked us down time and time again. In the second day the enemy will knock you down, and you will stay down. But in the third day, when the enemy knocks you down, you will get back up. Even though you are

* **wounded,**
* **scared,**
* **bruised,**
* **bleeding,**

One sound from the Lamb overcame three sounds of the rooster's crowing.

. . . you are going to get back up. When the enemy has knocked you down and starts to walk away, you are going to call out, "Where do you think you are going? Come back here. It's not over until I win." It's not over until you win, my friend. It's not over until God says it's over, and God is saying your time is about to begin right now.

THE PROPHETIC HOUR HAS ARRIVED

Woman of God . . . man of God . . . young person of the Lord—it is your hour to arise; it's not over until you win!

Peter thought it was over when the rooster crowed three times. But the Lamb spoke one time.

The Lamb said, "It is finished! I don't care what the rooster crowed . . . I don't care what the devil said. I don't care if he said it three times." The Lamb spoke one time, *and God said, "It is finished!"*

The sacrifice is finished. It is our time to arise, for we are the Jacob generation.

* **We are the great deceivers.**

* **We are the ones who are going to deceive the enemy.**

178

* We are the silent ones who yet shout.

* We are the timid ones who have no fear.

* We are the humble ones who yet are priests and kings.

* We are the great enigmas of the third day.

Let us consider the verses:

Then Jacob was left alone; and a Man wrestled with him until the breaking of day. Now when He saw that He did not prevail against him, He touched the socket of his hip; and the socket of Jacob's hip was out of joint as He wrestled with him. And He said, "Let Me go, for the day breaks."

But he said, "I will not let You go unless You bless me!"

So He said to him, "What is your name?"

He said, "Jacob."

And He said, "Your name shall no longer be called Jacob, but Israel; for you have struggled with God and with men, and have prevailed."

Then Jacob asked, saying, "Tell me Your name, I pray."

And He said, "Why is it that you ask about My name?" And He blessed him there.

So Jacob called the name of the place Peniel: "For I have seen God face to face, and my life is preserved." Just as he crossed over Penuel the sun rose on him, and he limped on his hip.

—Genesis 32:24–31

179

JACOB GENERATION PRINCIPLES

The story of Jacob's wrestling match in Scripture reveals important principles for the Third Day Jacob generation.

Let's take a closer look at some of these principles.

Wrestling before fighting

Jacob wrestled with God. Before we fight with the devil we must first wrestle with God. The devil has defeated many in the first and second days because they never wrestled with God first. When we wrestle with God, we do not defeat God. We are defeated in God. Once we are defeated in God and are consumed with His presence, power and anointing, we are prepared to move outside of God to face the enemy and defeat him. If we have first wrestled with God, then when we arrive at the enemies' camp to fight him, we need to tell him, "I can defeat you because I have wrestled with God, and I received my blessing; I have the power and the anointing to defeat you."

Third Day abandonment

Then Jacob was left alone . . . —GENESIS 32:24

Jacob was left alone. You will never receive the Third Day Jacob anointing with its limp, ladder, name and nation until you are left alone. You have been surrounded for too long.

* **You have been around people for too long.**

* **You have had access to your security blanket for too long.**

* **You have received acknowledgment and recognition from those around you for too long.**

You have never been left alone. That is why God makes sure that in the third day there comes a time when you are going to be left alone. I speak prophetically to you, friend, that there are those around you who will leave you and forsake you.

Understand that every time the world leaves you, God picks you up.

When your mother leaves you, God is your comforter. When your father leaves you, God is your provider. When everyone around you forsakes you, the Lord will pick you up.

When my father and my mother forsake me, then the LORD will take care of me.
—PSALM 27:10

Third Day daybreak

. . . and a Man wrestled with him until the breaking of day.—GENESIS 32:24

Jacob and his opponent fought until daybreak. **We must understand that "joy cometh in the morning" (Ps. 30:5, KJV). Your life may be dark right now, but the sun is about to rise. There might not be a star in the sky, but there is a star in your heart. In the midst of your darkness, there is a light. This is your day of rejoicing . . . your joy comes in the morning. It is an unexplainable joy. The kingdom of God is not meat or drink—it is righteousness, peace and joy in the Holy Spirit.**

For the kingdom of God is not meat and drink; but righteousness, and peace, and joy in the Holy Ghost.—ROMANS 14:17, KJV

181

Third Day perseverance

Now when He saw that He did not prevail against him, He touched the socket of his hip; and the socket of Jacob's hip was out of joint as He wrestled with him.—GENESIS 32:25

Jacob was already hurt, but he continued to wrestle.

* **You may be hurt, but you must keep on praising.**

* **You may be down, but you must keep on running.**

* **You may be sad, but you must keep on smiling.**

* **Don't stop. Don't quit. He who overcomes shall receive a new name.**

He who has an ear, let him hear what the Spirit says to the churches. To him who overcomes I will give some of the hidden manna to eat. And I will give him a white stone, and on the stone a new name written which no one knows except him who receives it.—REVELATION 2:17

God gives the Third Day Jacob generation a new name . . . a new identity. This name is reserved for all who overcome. Keep on fighting. Don't stop. Don't quit. Don't give up!

Third Day determination

And He said, "Let Me go, for the day breaks." But he said, "I will not let You go unless You bless me."—GENESIS 32:26

182

Jacob's opponent said, "Let Me go." But Jacob reply was, "I won't stop until You bless me.

* **"I won't stop praising until You bless me;**

* **"I won't stop fasting, praying and seeking You until You bless me;**

* **"I won't stop doing anything until You bless me."**

What is the reason we don't stop? It is because we want God to bless us at all times. We must say to God,

✳ **"I am going to continue praising;**

✳ **"I am going to continue worshiping;**

✳ **"I am going to continue praying;**

✳ **"I am going to continue eating Your Word, living Your Word, exercising Your Word and executing Your Word."**

We need a Third Day determination! We should yell out to God, "No, I will not let You go until You bless me." In the third day we cannot let go of God. We can let go of everything else, but not God.

The enemy will never be able to take the Holy Spirit away from you. He will never be able to take away your Jesus. But he has the power to destroy the things in your life. He can hurt and bruise the things in your life.

✳ **He might take away your church.**
✳ **He might take away your ministry.**
✳ **He might take away your fame and popularity.**
✳ **He might take away your car and your home.**
✳ **He might even take away a family member.**

But there are some thing that the devil can never take away.

✳ **He cannot take away your Jesus.**

✳ **He cannot take away the Holy Spirit.**

✳ **He cannot take away the anointing of God upon your life.**

✳ **He cannot take away the divine, eternal things.**

183

You are a Jacob participant in the Jacob generation. You represent the Third Day generation. You possess the Jacob generation characteristics.

Third Day royalty

> *And He said, "Your name shall no longer be Jacob, but Israel; for you have struggled with God and with men, and have prevailed."*
>
> —GENESIS 32:28

In this principle the angel calls you a prince. God is calling you a prince. It is your time to rise up as a Third Day king. Arise; your time has arrived to be lifted up to live in His sight as a Third Day king.

* **Stop following this world.**
* **Start ruling right now.**
* **Rule and reign in the name of Jesus.**

A time of power, promotion and possession has come to your life. This is your hour. Jacob, it is time to arise. You have power with God and with men. The Lord is telling you that in the Third Day anointing we will have power with both God and with men.

FOUR JACOB BLESSINGS

The Jacob generation is the only generation that will live in His sight. There are four things that God gave Jacob. These four things exist right now in the third day. As you read this book, God is giving you four powerful anointings, four powerful outpourings. They are the same as the four things God gave Jacob.

* **A limp—the blessing scar**
* **A ladder—the vision**
* **A name—the identity**
* **A nation—the place of destiny**

184

The limp *engages* the blessing scar, the ladder *enriches* the vision, the name *empowers* you through identity and the nation *enhances* you through destiny.

It is God who engages, empowers, enriches and enhances our generation. God engages, empowers, enriches and enhances you right now! God gives you a limp, a ladder, a name and a nation.

The limp

Jacob, arise; your third day has come. You have fought with God. You have wrestled with God, and you have won. When Jacob fought with God, he was left with a blessing *and a scar.* There are good scars, scars that move you and inspire you. There are blessings, good blessings that move you. First and second day blessings move you and get you to shout, twitch, jerk and dance. But Third Day blessings leave a scar.

You need a Third Day blessing in your life. That Third Day blessing is going to leave you a scar—but that scar is the mark of Jesus.

> *From now on let no one trouble me, for I bear in my body the marks of the Lord Jesus.*—GALATIANS 6:17

When you fight with God, you walk out of that fight wounded—bearing the marks of Christ. But with Christ's wounds, you are complete before the enemy.

185

With the wound of the Lord upon your life, you can exercise a Jacob anointing. You possess the Third Day blessing scar. The limp is the blessing scar. You can assert to those who question you about that limp, "I wrestled with God. The devil didn't mess me up—the devil can't mess me up. I wrestled with God, and I won."

When you are wounded with Christ, you are whole before the enemy.

We need to change our thinking . . . stop the victimization mentality that blames everything on the experiences of the past. Convert all the fuel from the past, and gas up your engines with it now, in the present and in the future. Tell those you meet, "All those tragedies I went through . . . all of those days I cried . . . all my suffering . . . they are my blessing scars. Those scars mean that I fought with God, and I won. I am a blessed Third Day member of the Jacob generation. I am a blessed, foot-stomping, throat-yelling, blood-washed, saved, sanctified, Spirit-filled, son of the Lord. I sing an apostolic, prophetic, devil-binding, demon-crushing, Third Day Jesus freak song. I am a Third Day Jacob generation participant.

* "I have Jacob's limp.
* "I am Jacob's limp.
* "I carry Jacob's limp.

"I have a blessing scar that no one will be able to take away."

In the third day you will live in His sight, and when God shows you His scars, you will show Him yours. You will say, "God, I know You have scars. Let me show You the scar I have—I look just like You!

* "Show me Your scar, and I'll show You mine.

* "Show me Your battle wound, and I'll show You my battle wound.

* "Show me Your medal, and I'll show You mine."

The ladder

When he [Jacob] came to a place, he spent the night there because

186

the sun had set. He found a [rock] and laid his head on it to go to sleep. Jacob dreamed that there was a ladder resting on the earth and reaching up into heaven, and he saw angels of God going up and coming down the ladder. Then Jacob saw the LORD standing above the ladder, and he said, "I am the LORD, the God of Abraham your grandfather, and the God of Isaac. I will give you and your descendants the land on which you are now sleeping. Your descendants will be as many as the dust of the earth. They will spread west and east, north and south, and all the families of the earth will be blessed through you and your descendants. I am with you and will protect you everywhere you go and will bring you back to this land. I will not leave you until I have done what I have promised you."

Then Jacob woke from his sleep and said, "Surely the LORD is in this place, but I did not know it." He was afraid and said, "This place frightens me! It is surely the house of God and the gate of heaven."

Jacob rose early in the morning and took the [rock] he had slept on and set it up on its end. Then he poured olive oil on top of it. At first, the name of that city was Luz, but Jacob named it Bethel.

Then Jacob made a promise. He said, "I want God to be with me and to protect me on this journey. I want him to give me food to eat and clothes to wear so I will be able to return in peace to my father's house. If the LORD does these things, he will be my God. This [rock] which I have set up on its end will be the house of God. And I will give God one-tenth of all he gives me."

—*GENESIS 28:11–22, NCV*

The ladder means *vision*. God gives this to the Third Day generation of Jacob. We have a vision that no one has ever seen before. God has given us the ladder of vision.

187

Have you failed at fully comprehending the destiny God has for you? Have you been unable to see further ahead in your life? You need to use the ladder to climb out of that circumstance.

 * **Climb out of your despair.**

 * **Climb out of your loneliness.**

 * **Climb out of your depression.**

 * **Climb out of the second day and climb into the third day.**

Jacob was lying on the rock when he saw a ladder and angels moving up and down the ladder. The angels are coming down with your blessings. At the top of the ladder, Jacob saw the glory of God. Now is the time for you to put your head upon the rock to catch the vision of the ladder.

The rock is an uncomfortable place. Jacob could have put his head upon the sand, but he put it upon the rock. Christianity is uncomfortable. The third day will be uncomfortable for many because it requires laying your head upon the rock.

In an earlier chapter we talked about climbing the mountain and standing upon the rock. But here, where did Jacob rest? Where do you rest? You rest upon the rock. You place your head upon Jesus, the supernatural rock. When you put your head upon Jesus, it is uncomfortable for the flesh. But there

188

The ladder is used to climb out of situations. Use your Jacob's ladder to climb out of your misery and despair.

you will see the ladder. The only way to see the ladder is to rest upon the rock. There you will receive the vision.

It is your hour . . . your time . . . to ascend into God's holy hill by using Jacob's ladder. Climb into His presence . . . climb into His glory . . . climb into the upper room . . . climb into the fullness of everything He has pre-destined for you. **Right now, climb into your promise . . . climb into your promotion . . . climb into your position . . . climb into your possession. Use the ladder in Jesus' name.**

The name

> *And Jacob asked him, and said, Tell me, I*
> *pray thee, thy name. And he said, Wherefore*
> *is it that thou dost ask after my name? And*
> *he blessed him there.* —GENESIS 32:29, KJV

The Third Day name is no other name but the name of Jesus. Jacob asked the name of his opponent. Although the angel did not give Jacob His name, Jacob moved into a Third Day revelation. Jacob was ahead of himself—he did not comprehend the importance of his question, but he received the benefits of that name just for asking.

Jacob wasn't asking for just any name. He was asking the name above all names. The name to whom every knee shall bow and every tongue shall confess. **The only name given unto man through which salvation comes to all mankind. The name that is excellent and majestic. He wanted THE NAME!**

189

The name of the Lord is a strong tower into which the righteous run (Prov. 18:10). It is a name above all other names. Jacob wanted to know the name, but he couldn't know the name yet—it wasn't his time.

But we have the name that Jacob was not able to receive. We have the name that Jacob was not allowed to hear. **We have the name, and not only do we hear the name—not only do we know the name—but we also have that name written in our hearts. It is the name of Jesus Christ.**

Jacob received a blessing just because he asked for that name. Do you understand that the moment you ask for the name, He will bless you? His name shall be called "Wonderful, Counselor, Mighty God, Everlasting Father, Prince of Peace" (Isa. 9:6).

If you know His name, He knows your name.

> ✳ You call Him *Father;* He calls you *son.*
> ✳ You call Him *King;* He calls you *prince.*
> ✳ You call Him *Savior;* He calls you *saint.*
> ✳ You call Him *Healer;* He calls you *healed.*
> ✳ You call Him *Deliverer;* He calls you *delivered.*

He calls you a child of God. Just as He blessed Jacob when he asked His name, when you ask His name, He will bless you right there.

> ✳ Right there in your pain He is about to bless you.
>
> ✳ Right there in your hell God is blessing you.
>
> ✳ Right there in your suffering God is blessing you.
>
> ✳ Right there in your circumstance God is blessing you.
>
> ✳ Right there in your struggle, in your war, God is blessing you.

God changed Jacob's name to Israel. God wants to change your name from

✳ defeat to victory,
✳ hell to heaven,
✳ despair to hope,
✳ emptiness to fulfillment,
✳ darkness to light,
✳ bland to seasoned.

When you wrestle with God, your name will be changed to Israel. God is the God of Israel. He is your God. God has many names:

✳ *Jehovah-jireh*—the Lord Our Provider
✳ *Jehovah-nissi*—the Lord Our Banner
✳ *Jehovah-rophe*—the Lord Our Healer
✳ *Jehovah-shammah*—the Lord Is Present
✳ *Adonai*—the Lord
✳ *El Shaddai*—the Almighty God
✳ *The Great I AM*

But you also have a name in the third day. You are a chosen generation. You are a

✳ column of iron,
✳ wall of bronze,
✳ chosen people,
✳ royal priesthood,
✳ holy nation,
✳ people belonging to God,
✳ temple of the Holy Spirit,
✳ salt of the earth,
✳ light of the world,
✳ fortified city,
✳ city upon the hill.

191

You are all of those things—and more. You are a prince. You are a king. You are a holy priesthood. In the third day your name changes. Your identity changes.

The nation

God told Jacob, "Now I give you the nations." God gives you destiny, friend. The Third Day anointing exhibits and executes global dominance. The Third Day church utilizes technology and science to impact the entire global spectrum.

* ✱ **God gives you your family.**
* ✱ **God gives you your neighborhood.**
* ✱ **God gives you your community.**
* ✱ **God gives you your city.**
* ✱ **God gives you your state.**
* ✱ **God gives you your province.**
* ✱ **God gives you your region.**
* ✱ **God gives you your nation.**
* ✱ **God gives you the world.**

Arise, Jacob, arise. Let me make a special note here—the Jacob spirit is a youthful spirit—*one that has nothing to do with age*. God is rejuvenating us to prepare us to walk with the limp, to climb the ladder, to emulate our new name and to declare victory over the nations.

God is placing within each Third Day worshiper, regardless of age, a youthful anointing. God assigns characteristics to us that will be evident in our lives as a result of this anointing of spiritual youth. He says we will:

192

> . . . *soar on wings like eagles.*—Isaiah 40:31, NIV

You are an eagle, my friend—not a chicken. We are to soar on eagles' wings, see with eagle vision. We will see things far into the future. We will see prophetically.

> *Your sons and your daughters shall prophesy, your young men shall see visions.*
> —Acts 2:17

Seeing things that have never been seen before requires eagle vision.

With our anointing we will also be strengthened to carry off the dead:

> *Then the young men came in and, finding her dead, carried her out and buried her beside her husband.—Acts 5:10, NIV*

When Ananias and Sapphira lied against the Holy Spirit, they fell dead. The young people were called to carry out the dead. Friend, the Third Day Christian will carry out the dead. Those who have received an anointing of youthful spirit will carry out the dead—dead praise, dead worship, dead preaching, dead teaching, dead religion and traditions of man. All these things need to be buried.

There are many dead things in the church that need to be carried out and buried.

The Jacob generation will also trample over Satan in the power of God:

> *I write to you, young men, because you have overcome the evil one.*
> —1 John 2:13, NIV

193

> *"Lord, even the demons are subject to us in Your name." And He said to them . . . "I give you the authority to trample on serpents and scorpions and over all the power of the enemy, and nothing shall by any means hurt you."—Luke 10:17–19*

We are the Jacob generation. We possess the limp, the ladder, the name and the nation. We live in His sight. We will rise up in His sight. Arise, Third Day Jacob generation. Let the world see your limp, ladder, name and nation.

Are you Third Day?

Living in His Sight: Third Day Instruments of Change

Change, *change*, **change.** In any worthwhile human endeavor, one requires a larger spiritual vision, which constructs the theoretical framework in which a person addresses all concrete situations in order to make crucial decisions.

This larger spiritual vision, in the end, dictates the paradigm we create as Christians. Within that theoretical paradigm, situations and unsatisfactory results provoke the necessity for change. In the past, any change in the Christian forum was synonymous with reformation or revival. Yet, in the latter part of the twentieth century and now in the early part of the twenty-first century, a new phraseology has arisen with a corresponding change process that distinguishes itself from all prior reformed efforts.

> The phrase *third day* brings about a different approach in the transformation of churches and Christian believers as a whole.

Becoming third day requires all parts of the Christian Spirit-filled system to change, starting with believers and leaders and progressing up through miry bureaucratic layers. Two key features distinguish third day from previous revival efforts:

1 *It is driven by a focus on the person of Jesus*, based on the premise that all Third Day Christians can and must worship at higher levels.

2 *It is a long-term commitment to fundamental, systematic change.*

I have been able to experience this Third Day paradigm shift. It has impacted

* my church,
* my prayer life,
* my worship,
* my existence.

At Third Day Worship Center where I am presently the senior pastor, we are beginning the implementation phase of our Third Day Project. I have been whole-heartedly involved in all aspects of our reformation, though at times I have been dissatisfied with some of the results. My objectives are to

* evaluate the current standing and stance of the Spirit-filled, full-gospel, evangelical Christian church, and

* develop a comprehensive improvement plan, utilizing *the third day* as a phase that incorporates the vision.

The plan is initiated by a sincere invitation to change under the authority and the anointing of the Holy Spirit, a change that gives the following:

* Flexibility
* Knowledge
* Time

These three elements will result in a designed plan, which such a process demands. The Third Day plan includes

* the statement of a problem,
* the identification of activities needed to solve the problem,
* the listings of the individuals or groups to be involved in transforming a church, a ministry or a believer into a Third Day worshiper,
* the timeline for implementation.

THE STATEMENT OF A PROBLEM

It is important to know that change for the sake of change is not only useless, but it also can become counter-productive. Therefore, the identification of the problem that motivates the necessity for change becomes of utmost importance. Problems within the Spirit-filled, full-gospel, evangelical body of Christ coincide with many similar problems that have existed in mainline denominations throughout the past few hundred years:

* Low attendance
* Low membership status
* High impersonality
* High sense of not belonging

In fact, an undeniable truth exists in the predominance of pastor-centered worship, leadership, work and relationship with Christ.

197

The need to shift to prophetic preaching and teaching of the Word of God that is intertwined with the delivery of information for the development of intellectual skills such as critical thinking, along with a need to help worshipers construct their own relationships from meaningful Christ-centered experiences, cannot be ignored.

We have also failed to meet the cognitive and intellectual needs of minorities and culturally different worshipers. For example, many of our congregations on Sunday morning do not reflect the demographic diversities of the cities in which we are located. The vast majority of people who come to our altars for conversion eventually drop out. In fact, a need exists to reduce the fragmentation of doctrinal teachings in order to help worshipers make important connections to real spiritual phenomenon.

The Word needs to come to life and be both applicable and practical for ministering to

* the mind,
* the hand,
* the heart,
* the intellect,
* the emotion,
* the spirit.

Finally, we have failed to provide mature nurturing experiences that better prepare worshipers in the transition to the ministry world after discipleship. Let me explain. We have done a remarkable job in filling our church with converts, when in reality our number one objective is to fill our church with

* disciples,
* worshipers,
* apostles,
* prophets,
* pastors,
* evangelists,
* teachers,
* exhorters,
* miracle workers.

We bring them in as

　　✳ **undesirables,**
　　✳ **sinners,**
　　✳ **shamed,**
　　✳ **rejects,**
　　✳ **the lowest of them all.**

Then the living and active Word of God reaches them!
We prepare them, and we commission them. The only
possible way a Third Day church ministry or life can execute such a mission is by imparting a vision that will provoke a mission. This imparted vision will give birth to a
mission, which will eventually lead to a commission.

　　✳ **Vision: A Third Day Christian has a vision.**
　　✳ **Mission: A Third Day Christian is involved in**
　　　 a mission.
　　✳ **Commission: A Third Day Christian is under**
　　　 a great commission.

The Third Day plan must address the core problems of a
group of believers I call Third Day dropouts. These individuals have withdrawn because of their feelings of disen-
franchisement and alienation. To reengage these dropouts
for God, we must develop a way to assess how our congregations perceive their worship experiences. As we discover
how to move beyond second day problems of a lack of discipleship, lack of self-conceptualization and a degree of dis-
satisfaction with the worship experience as a whole, we will
be able to reach these dropouts and lift them to dynamic
Third Day spiritual life. A Third Day ministry . . . a Third
Day church . . . Third Day believers . . . are not an island
in themselves. A Third Day worshiper is not hidden in his
prayer closet preoccupied with his personal life.

199

Organizations in the third day need to set aside short-
term, antiquated layers of bureaucracy. Plans need to be

A Third Day worshiper strives continuously to engage, empower, enrich and enhance his family, household, neighborhood, community, city, state, nation and world for Jesus Christ.

implemented that will engage individuals for God, involve them in discipleship and provide them with the pragmatic spiritual experiences and connections necessary to equip them for ministry in their world. Much of this can be done through interdisciplinary teachings and the establishment of Third Day partnerships. Pastors, ministers, leaders and worshipers need to build relationships that are

✳ **above religion,**
✳ **above programs,**
✳ **above ministry.**

There should be dynamic teamwork between worshipers, staff and leaders who will develop expectations for all worshipers around them. This team can provide a common language for change and a safe level of ambiguity that will allow the team to make any necessary course corrections during the journey from first and second day life to supernatural, revolutionary Third Day living.

200   The pastor is the individual with a vision. He or she articulates that vision and provides the physical, relational, logistical and motivational framework for the realization of the vision.

The pastor must be the cultural, symbolic, instructional, technical, spiritual and human leader of the church before becoming the leader of change.

Thus, somewhere between wide-eyed Pollyannaism and

close-minded cynicism, this pastor charts his course to the wild sea of revival . . . to raising up and living in God's sight in the third day despite the risk. I have decided to chart the course on the ship called *Third Day*, with the end result of enriching, enhancing and empowering all people for the honor and glory of Jesus Christ.

In this first stage of learning to state the problem, we must wrestle with the question of why the church . . . this church . . . your church . . . has not grown.

* ✳ **What are the reasons that change has not occurred?**
* ✳ **What are the elements necessary for change?**
* ✳ **What are the prime issues my church must face?**
* ✳ **What are the most outstanding concerns hindering change?**

What must be done to change a second day worshiper . . . a second day church . . . into a Third Day church and a Third Day worshiper?

IDENTIFICATION OF ACTIVITIES NEEDED TO SOLVE THE PROBLEM

After you have taken the time to analyze thoroughly the question, "What is the problem hindering me . . . my family . . . my church . . . from becoming a dynamic Third Day worshiper and church?", you will move forward to creating a solution to that problem. During this second stage of the Third Day plan, you should consider each of the following questions:

* ✳ **What data do I need to gather in order to create a solution?**

201

✳ **What activities do I have to undertake?**
✳ **Do I survey the congregation?**
✳ **Do I survey myself?**
✳ **Do I survey the community?**
✳ **How does the community perceive our church and our community?**
✳ **How do the people around me perceive me?**
✳ **How do my wife, my husband, my kids and the rest of my family perceive me?**
✳ **What does my neighbor say about me?**
✳ **What testimony am I giving?**
✳ **What glory, what presence, what anointing am I giving out?**

As you consider these questions in the third day, you will find that the manifold wisdom of God will lead you in answering such questions. The fact of the matter is, human intellect, organized planning and pragmatic application will not suffice in the third day. The apostle Paul descriptively stated in his first letter to the church of Corinth that his approach was not based on "human wisdom, but in demonstration of the Spirit and of power" (1 Cor. 2:4). He later states it is the Spirit of God who searches the deep things of God (v. 10). If we intend to identify the necessary activities needed to solve problems, then we must go beyond the superficiality of our humanity and endeavor into the true identity of our spirituality.

202

You may ask, "Is there not some type of systematic guideline to follow in order to assist me in my problem solving?" The answer is yes. But the activity needed goes beyond our own interpretation of what will work considering all variables and formulas available for analysis. The answer in the third day awaits you in three areas of your life:

* **Your time in God's Word**
* **Your time in prayer to God**
* **Your time in consecration to God**

Therefore, you must learn to depend on God to supply you with the answers that only He can provide as a result of your relationship with Him. Will you use guidelines, parameters, planning, organization, implementation and other tools to solve your problems? Yes. But they will stem from the Spirit of God—not from man's idea.

LISTING OF GROUPS OR INDIVIDUALS TO BE INVOLVED IN TRANSFORMATION

Whom do I want to be involved with me in becoming third day? Who can help me to become a Third Day worshiper, a Third Day church or group?

Third Day criteria for partnering and networking with other Third Day believers include believers who are

* **meek as lambs and bold as lions,**
* **soldiers of the Lord of Hosts,**
* **transformed like water into wine,**
* **founded on principles of truth,**
* **unashamed to sound the alarm,**
* **united despite cultures, nationalities and ethnicity,**
* **devoted to reach the mark,**
* **determined to climb the heights,**
* **focused on the promise,**
* **willing to change,**
* **able to rise from a fall,**
* **destined to win with Christ!**

203

Why do these individuals need to be involved? Quite

possibly, you may want to engage some people who are from other churches. The time for individual men to build empires around their charisma or personality has ended. In the third day we will partner together and build the kingdom of Jesus Christ. Your Third Day partners will be one with you, and you will be one with them. They will have your heart, and you will have their heart. They will have your promise, and you will have their promise. Why? Because the third day is for everyone who desires to be one with God.

I refuse to build Third Day Worship Center in Staten Island, New York. I will build the kingdom of Jesus Christ, and He will build our local church. If we focus on building the kingdom, He will focus on building our local churches.

TIMELINE FOR IMPLEMENTATION

Here are the changes that I want to see in the next year that will indicate a move from second day to third day.

* Our Third Day vision must be matched with a Third Day constitution.
* Our Third Day spirit must be founded on a Third Day bureaucracy.
* Our Third Day preaching must be accompanied with Third Day praise and worship.

204

Every element within the church or individual must be third day. Third Day prophetic prayer must include prophetic worship. **My proposed timeline for implementing my Third Day vision needs to be balanced. I must detail what actions and leadership approaches will be required for the plan to succeed. Third Day living must be evident in every phase of my life and church.**

THIRD DAY PLAN DYNAMICS

When the problem has been stated, the solutions identified, the individuals committed and the timeline implemented, the Third Day plan will be ready. As we move forward into Third Day living, the following dynamics should be a part of that life.

Third Day prophecy

Third Day worshipers exemplify the prophetic. The prophetic goes beyond one of the ordained gifts of the Holy Spirit. The prophetic anointing and the prophetic spirit are a fulfillment of that which Joel prophesied:

> *And it shall come to pass afterward that I will pour out My Spirit on all flesh; your sons and your daughters shall prophesy, your old men shall dream dreams, your young men shall see visions.* —JOEL 2:28

There are a number of very important things about prophecies, visions and dreams. Our psalmist, Peter De Jesus, articulated and expressed revelation regarding prophecy, vision and dreams.

✳ **A prophecy is the spoken Word of God.**
✳ **A vision is the visible Word of God.**
✳ **A dream is the sown Word of God.**

205

God gives you a prophetic word, which becomes a vision, which becomes a dream in order to lead you into the fullness of God for your life.

Therefore, when we combine these three elements in the third day, we begin to live in His sight! But it all starts off with the prophetic—the voice of God—for you and me.

The first thing the apostles began to do after the outpouring of the Holy Spirit in the upper room on the Day of Pentecost was to proclaim the wonders of God to the people in their own languages. They spoke on behalf of God. They moved in the prophetic. In order for our implementations to effect Third Day change, every Third Day believer, worshiper, church, ministry, man, woman and young person must have and must be flowing with prophecy, visions and dreams.

> ✳ **We must be a prophetic generation.**
> ✳ **We must be a prophetic people.**
> ✳ **We must prophesy.**
> ✳ **We must engage in prophetic prayer.**
> ✳ **We must praise and worship under a prophetic anointing.**

We need to go beyond just asking for things. We need to prophesy over entire cities. We need to prophesy over our neighborhoods and over our families. **Let the second day be the last day you cried out for the salvation of your children.** Let the third day be the day when you enter the bedroom of your child and prophesy over your son, prophesy over your daughter, **prophesy over your alcoholic spouse, prophesy over your teenager who is using drugs or rebelling and see the power of God move through the prophetic word.**

206

In the third day, prophets of God must arise. In the third day, men and women of God, as prophets, arise. Arise and prophesy. Arise and declare. Arise and decree.

Third Day visions

Undoubtedly one of the most misunderstood concepts in the Spirit-filled body of Christ today is that of visions. So many erroneous, carnal, left-winged visions have been expressed and given out that there is so much skepticism and agnosticism. Yet God still gives visions to His servants. Men and women of God in the third day have visions.

The vision of Jacob (Gen. 28)—In the unfolding of this vision, we can see each of the following elements:

* Step-by-step praise
* Step-by-step worship
* Step-by-step prayer
* Step-by-step Bible study
* Step-by-step prophecy
* Step-by-step song of the Lord
* Step-by-step rejoicing

The vision of Isaiah (Isa. 6)—This vision reveals that when the king died, the prophet saw the Lord.

* When your king dies, you will see the Lord.
* When the king of this earth dies, you will see the King of glory arise.
* When the king dies, you will see the Lord high and lifted up and the angels crying, "Holy, holy, holy."

If you want to see yourself flying, the king must die. If you want to see yourself going from one level of glory to another, the king must die. If you want the coal of fire to pierce your lips, to sanctify them and give you a fiery prophetic word in the third day, the king must die.

207

The vision of Stephen (Acts 7)—Stephen saw a vision while being persecuted. Saul of Tarsus was there as a witness as Stephen, in the midst of persecution, saw the Lord. In the midst of persecution, you will see the Lord—not sitting down to receive you, but standing up to honor you.

Third Day dreams

Joseph had dreams. Daniel had dreams. Paul had dreams. And friend, you need to arise with prophecy, visions and dreams.

Prophecy, visions and dreams will enable you to provoke a change in your life, in your ministry, in your family, in your home, in your anointing and in your worship.

A DAY IN THE LIFE OF A THIRD DAY WORSHIPER

3:00 A.M.

I am unable to sleep, uncomfortable with my humanity, with the weariness of the daily grind. No other choice, no other alternative but to arise and to lie prostrate before the Lord and intercede for those who are hurting. I know my intercession must go beyond some type of psychotherapeutic, psychological manipulation . . . go beyond mere words. I understand that without a doubt every word in my mouth has power to create and power to destroy.

There is a Genesis and Revelation, knowing that whatsoever I ask in His name He shall do. So I intercede . . . I plead . . . I cry . . . and I weep. Knowing that He hears me and executes accordingly, I pray diligently and earnestly. I begin by praying in my language and understanding. Then suddenly, it goes away, and I am praying in another language. Unintelligible to me, those prayers provoke the angels of glory to descend with sharpened swords to engage in battle against the principalities of the air and the powers that govern those around us. I intercede. I plead prophetically under the anointing as I use scripture upon scripture.

I declare it, proclaim it, release it and know it to be true.

208

✳ When my words fail, His words will succeed.
✳ When my efforts fall short, His Spirit will take it to the ultimate place.

After all the prayers, all the shouting, all the worshiping, all the intercessions, all the tongues—after all, at the end—I have nothing more and nothing less to say, but . . . **Your will be done!**

6:00 A.M.

Waking up, before heading for the shower, the first thing I do is hit the ground—as in some type of Marine ritual. Not a push up, but a push down with my body. I extend the royal diadem, crowning Him Lord of all. I lie and recognize His sovereignty, His reign, and declare, "O Lord our Lord, how majestic is Thy name through all the earth. How excellent is Thy name. The heavens and the earth together proclaim how excellent is Thy name."

By the end of that day I will make it to the holy of holies.

I arise from the floor and go into the shower, where I begin my praise and worship. Then, in my automobile . . . in the public transit system . . . in whatever vehicle I use . . . I am in the glory. I long to go deeper. I may begin at the outer court, but my destiny is nothing less than the holy of holies.

209

I press on. Daily, somehow, somewhere, my mission is to break through the crowd . . . break through the masses . . . to enter into His gates with thanksgiving and into His courts with praise. **I go through the outer court, the inner court and finally enter into the holy of holies. The veil has been broken, but I must daily pierce through.**

I must pierce through

* my shortcomings,
* my flesh,
* my temperament,
* my stubbornness,
* my pride.

I struggle daily. Therefore, I fight daily. Somewhere, somehow I must break through. On a daily basis—for a lifetime—the Third Day worshiper must go through the outer court and the inner court to enter the holy of holies.

12:00 P.M.

Here I am at lunch hour—praying in tongues, interceding, loosing the prophetic, prophesying over my workplace, making those around me understand they are blessed because I am blessed. They are blessed because

* I am carrying the glory,
* the glory of God resides within me,
* I am a child of the living God.

A Third Day worshiper worships and praises without ceasing. Regardless of my activity, the Holy Spirit intercedes through my continuous prayer. A Third Day worshiper goes beyond memorizing a scripture or two—a Third Day warrior lives in the Word, thrives on the Word and flies through the Word. I must not limit myself to revival. Revival is only for a season. After revival comes the raising up. After the raising up comes the act of living in His sight. **I want to go beyond "having" revival.** I want to live revival. I want to abide in revival. **I want to execute revival. I want to flow in revivial.**

I don't want merely to touch His glory—I want to live in His glory. I don't want just to experience a touch from God here and there—I want to become the touch of God.

210

Wherever I am, I am God's touch to others. I must be completely intertwined with God—but how can it be? Beyond understanding . . . beyond belief . . . beyond our hopes and our fears. My friend, there is a place.

My heart lives with one objective—I want to put a smile on the face of God.

How futile that sounds. How minuscule that portrays itself to be. Nevertheless, that is the greatest of challenges. For how can God be smiling while looking down on His creation—with hatred and bitterness disseminating from their mouths, hearts and hands toward each other?

✳ **How can God be smiling when His bride is divided?**

✳ **How can God be smiling when His children are at war?**

✳ **How can God be smiling when we have created an institutionalized environment rather than a living, powerful glory?**

✳ **How can God be smiling when genocide, suicide and random murders and killings exist in every city . . . in every social economic group . . . in every culture . . . in every background on this planet?**

✳ **How can God be smiling when His name is used in vain—minute by minute . . . second by second . . . hour by hour?**

✳ **How can God be smiling when men and women use His name for individual gain, convincing themselves they do it for the honor and glory of God?**

✳ How can God be smiling when we forget those who are hurting ... abandoned ... disenfranchised ... and alienated?

✳ How can God be smiling when we neglect those who are poor ... homeless ... needy ... unemployed ... orphaned ... widowed ... undesirable ... rejected ... and dying?

How can God be smiling?

At the end of the road, I am finally here before You to bring You joy ... to bring You peace. I am here to let You know that it was worth it!

Here I am, finally before Him, with one objective— to provoke Him to smile. Not as if I were some court jester in joyful exuberance attempting to provoke an emotion from God. **At times I am perplexed by the continuous bashing of emotionalism when our God is our divine embodiment of sacred emotion. God Himself smiles ... rejoices ... laughs ... weeps ... and cries.**

"Lord, my objective today is to put a smile upon Your face. Could it be, God, that You need a reason to laugh and rejoice?"

212

Are you Third Day?

Living
in His
Sight:
Third Day
Dust

Dust, *dust*, **dust.** Ashes to ashes, dust to dust. Look what God does with dust. We live in His sight as Third Day dust. We display the powerful relationship between the sovereign Creator of the universe and the minuscule particles of dust—you and I.

* ✳ God collected the dust from the earth in Genesis.
* ✳ God breathed upon the dust.
* ✳ And here we are today.

Look what God does with dust. He forms you. He forms me out of the dust of the earth.

> *The LORD God formed the man from the dust of the ground and breathed into his nostrils the breath of life, and the man became a living being.—GENESIS 2:7, NIV*

213

What does God accomplish with dust?

* ✳ He forms it into His image.
* ✳ He forms it into His likeness.

Not only did God form it into His image and likeness in the first day, but God also breathed upon that dust, creating life—the soul of man. God also makes something with dust in the third day. The Bible tells us about a man who was born blind; when Jesus Christ healed him, He spat on the ground, forming mud.

1 *God forms dust into His image and likeness.*

Then God said, "Let Us make man in Our image, according to Our likeness.—GENESIS 1:26

2 *He shakes off the dust.*

And whoever will not receive you nor hear your words, when you depart from that house or city, shake off the dust from your feet.—MATTHEW 10:14

3 *He makes miracles out of messes.*

When He had said these things, He spat on the ground and made clay with the saliva; and He anointed the eyes of the blind man with the clay.—JOHN 9:6

In the third day, God works with dust.

* **He collects dust.**
* **He spits on dust.**
* **He creates a miracle out of dust.**

214 He no longer breathes on dust—He spits on it. No longer is He giving out just His soul—He is giving out His water, His Spirit.

It might look like a mess, but it is actually a miracle! God is making a miracle out of the mess.

* **He creates a mud ball.**
* **He places it on your eyes.**
* **He makes a miracle out of it.**

God is making a miracle out of your mess—out of your circumstance . . . your marriage . . . your home . . . your finances . . . your body. It may look like a mess, but it is just a mud ball. God is spitting on the ground.

✳ **When God spits on humanity,**
✳ **when God incorporates His saliva,**
✳ **when God puts His taste,**
✳ **when God cultivates His flavor,**
✳ **when God imparts that which is inside of Him,**
✳ **when God places Himself upon you,**

. . . it may look like a mess in the beginning, but in the end, it is the miracle of God for your life. The upper room looked like a mess in its initial phase. It sounded like a mess. That is why many are still trying to understand this whole Spirit-filled movement. It looks messy. It looks awkward. It looks disorderly. But it is actually a miracle.

No longer is God imparting life through the soul; He is imparting life through the Spirit.

God makes a mud ball out of your mess and turns it into a miracle. Right now, God is placing a mud ball upon every aspect of your life. Your life may look chaotic and disorderly right now, but actually there is a miracle underneath that mess.

God writes on dust.

215

Jesus went to Mount Olives, but he was soon back in the Temple again. Swarms of people came to him. He sat down and taught them.

The religion scholars and Pharisees led in a woman who had been caught in an act of adultery. They stood her in plain sight of everyone and said, "Teacher, this woman was caught red-handed in the act of adultery. Moses, in the Law, gives orders to stone such persons. What do you say?" They were trying to trap him into saying something incriminating so that they could bring charges against him.

Jesus bent down and wrote with his finger in the dirt. They kept at him, badgering him. He straightened up and said, "The sinless one among you, go first: Throw the stone." Bending down again, he wrote some more in the dirt.

Hearing that, they walked away, one after another, beginning with the oldest. The woman was left alone. Jesus stood up and spoke to her. "Woman, where are they?" Does no one condemn you?"

"No one, Master."

"Neither do I," said Jesus. "Go on your way. From now on, don't sin."

—JOHN 8:1–11, THE MESSAGE

God writes on dust. We know this story about Jesus writing on dust. The Pharisees were ready to throw stones at this adulteress woman. But Jesus wrote on the dust. Why did He write on dust? Jesus wrote on dust regarding the woman. Why?

Jesus was writing about the woman because He was not in heaven to write in the Lamb's Book of Life.

Possibly Jesus wrote a Post-It note—"She is saved." Jesus sent an e-mail before there was e-mail. He was online before there was the Internet. **He faxed a memo—"She is Ours."** **He wrote on dust.**

216

Jesus wrote on humanity. Friend, He is writing on your humanity today. Although the Pharisees were accusing her, He ignored them.

God does not listen to the devil's trash talk against you, friend. He ignores it. Note that He did not write in the heavens...in the middle

God ignores the devil when he comes to accuse us.

places . . . in the palace . . . in the pinnacles of fame and popularity. God wrote on the ground.

> ✳ **When the world knocks you down,**
> ✳ **when the devil knocks you down,**
> ✳ **when your flesh knocks you down,**

. . . *Jesus is there to write on you again.* Just like a boxer knocked down to the ground, it is when you are your weakest that God makes you strong. It is on the ground that God writes a word upon your life. My friend, God is about to write upon your life today. You may have been grounded, but at the moment of your grounding, God writes upon you.

Oh, if the devil only knew that every time he grounds you, God writes a word upon your life. If he knew that, he would not have messed with you in the first place.

> ✳ **The Father wrote the Word with one finger.**
> ✳ **The Son wrote the Word with two hands.**
> ✳ **But the Holy Spirit writes the Word with fire.**

When the Holy Spirit writes upon your life, He writes with fire.

> ✳ **Fire burns.**
> ✳ **Fire penetrates.**
> ✳ **Fire is indiscernible.**

One can read the language of the Father. One can read 217 the language of the Son. But not just anyone can read the language of the Holy Spirit, for it is not a language discernible by man.

> ✳ **It is a heavenly language.**
> ✳ **It is a divine language.**
> ✳ **It is a powerful language.**

DIRT OR DUST?

We are no longer the dirt of the second day—the curse of the second day. We are not just any dust. We are blessed dust. We are not second day curses; we are Third Day blessings.

* **You are either living with a second day curse or a Third Day blessing.**

* **You are either living as dirt that failed or as dust that was written upon by the fire of the Holy Spirit.**

When you live in His sight, you live with a continuous blessing.

* **You may have been cursed with heart disease, but now you are blessed with *Jehovah-rophe*.**

* **You may have been cursed with poverty, but today you are blessed with *Jehovah-jireh*.**

* **You may have been cursed with turmoil, but today you are blessed with *Jehovah-shalom*.**

* **You may have been cursed with no identity, but today you are blessed with *Jehovah-nissi*.**

* **You may have been cursed with loneliness, but today you are blessed with *Jehovah-shammah*.**

* **You may have been cursed with unrighteousness, but today you are blessed with *Jehovah-tsidkenu*.**

* **You may have been cursed with weakness, but today you are blessed with *El Shaddai*.**

There are many curses out there, but the blood of Jesus Christ broke the curse.

> *Christ redeemed us from the curse of the law by becoming a curse for us, for it is written: "Cursed is everyone who is hung on a tree."*—GALATIANS 3:13, NIV

✳ **Get up and shout, the curse is broken.**
✳ **Get up and dance, the curse is broken.**
✳ **Get up and worship, the curse is broken.**

Mama was bound to it; Daddy was hooked by it; but now I am free from it.

When the curse is over, the blessing begins.

THE BLESSING ENTRANCE

You cannot live with your second day curse. You must live with a Third Day blessing.

There is a second day curse, and there is a Third Day blessing. In order for you to live in the Third Day blessing, you must come into your blessing through the blessing entrance.

> *Now the LORD had said to Abram: "Get out of your country, from your family and from your father's house, to a land that I will show you. I will make you a great nation; I will bless you and make your name great; and you shall be a blessing. I will bless those who bless you, and I will curse him who curses you; and in you all the families of the earth shall be blessed."*—GENESIS 12:1–3

219

Therefore, in order to come into your blessing, you must come out of your curse. Come out, come out wherever you are.

✳ **Noah came out of the ark.**
✳ **Moses came out of the desert.**
✳ **Jonah came out of the whale.**
✳ **John came out of the wilderness.**
✳ **Lazarus came out of the tomb.**
✳ **JESUS CHRIST CAME OUT OF THE GRAVE.**

Repeat after me: "I am coming out! I am coming out!" You must come out in order to come in.

Say it:

✳ **"I am coming out of sin.**
✳ **"I am coming out of poverty.**
✳ **"I am coming out of my flesh.**
✳ **"I am coming out of abuse.**
✳ **"I am coming out of victimization.**
✳ **"I am coming out of religion.**
✳ **"I am coming out of mediocrity.**
✳ **"I am coming out of complacency.**
✳ **"I am coming out of comfort.**
✳ **"I am coming out of pride.**
✳ **"I am coming out of envy.**
✳ **"I am coming out of lust.**
✳ **"I am coming out of jealousy.**
✳ **"I am coming out of hatred.**
✳ **"I am coming out of the second day.**
✳ **"I am coming into the third day!"**

Do something right now, my friend. Get up and look back. That is the last time you will ever look back.

For you have need of endurance, so that after you have done the will of God, you

220

may receive the promise: "For yet a little while, and He who is coming will come and will not tarry. Now the just shall live by faith; but if anyone draws back, My soul has no pleasure in him."—HEBREWS 10:36–38

From now on, you will always be looking forward.

* **Come out of your misery.**
* **Come out of your debt.**
* **Come out of your pain.**
* **Come into His glory.**
* **Come into the victory.**
* **Come into the anointing.**
* **Come into the cross.**
* **Come into the empty tomb.**
* **Come into the upper room.**
* **Come into the prophetic.**
* **Come into the song of the Lord.**
* **Come into the Word of almighty God.**
* **Come into sound doctrine.**
* **Come into the fullness of the river.**

Come into God's Third Day glory.

We are coming out of the second day, and we are going into the glory realm.

* **Come out of religion, and come into revival.**
* **Come out of religiosity, and come into the rising up.**
* **Come out of experiences, and come into living in His sight.**

221

WE'RE BLESSED!

Jesus said, "Before Abraham was, I AM." Before Abraham was blessed, I was already blessed. The blessing does not come from Abraham—the blessing comes from Jesus Christ.

* **Before you were sick, He already healed you.**
* **Before you were down, He already lifted you up.**
* **Before you sinned, He already forgave you.**
* **Before you were destroyed, He already repaired you.**
* **Before Abraham was, I AM, hallelujah!**

Blessed is the man

Who walks not in the counsel of the ungodly,

Nor stands in the path of sinners,

Nor sits in the seat of the scornful;

But his delight is in the law of the LORD,

And in His law he meditates day and night.

He shall be like a tree

Planted by the rivers of water,

That brings forth its fruit in its season,

Whose leaf also shall not wither;

And whatever he does shall prosper.

The ungodly are not so,

But are like the chaff which the wind drives away.

Therefore the ungodly shall not stand in the judgment,

Nor sinners in the congregation of the righteous.

For the LORD knows the way of the righteous,

But the way of the ungodly shall perish.

—PSALM 1:1–6

You are blessed. You possess the blessing of Jesus from Matthew 5.

When Jesus saw his ministry drawing huge crowds, he climbed a hillside. Those who were apprenticed to him, the committed, climbed

222

with him. Arriving at a quiet place, he sat down and taught his climbing companions. This is what he said:

"You're blessed when you're at the end of your rope. With less of you there is more of God and his rule.

"You're blessed when you feel you've lost what is most dear to you. Only then can you be embraced by the One most dear to you.

"You're blessed when you're content with just who you are—no more, no less. That's the moment you find yourselves proud owners of everything that can't be bought.

"You're blessed when you've worked up a good appetite for God. He's food and drink in the best meal you'll ever eat.

"You're blessed when you care. At the moment of being 'care-full,' you find yourselves cared for.

"You're blessed when you get your inside world—your mind and heart—put right. Then you can see God in the outside world.

"You're blessed when your commitment to God provokes persecution. The persecution drives you even deeper into God's kingdom.

"Not only that—count yourselves blessed every time people put you down or throw you out or speak lies about you to discredit me. What it means is that the truth is too close for comfort and they are uncomfortable. You can be glad when that happens—give a cheer, even!—for though they don't like it, I do! And all heaven applauds. And know that you are in good company. My prophets and witnesses have always gotten into this kind of trouble."

223

—*Matthew 5:1–12, The Message*

＊ **There are blessings you come into—Abraham (Gen. 12:1–3).**
＊ **Blessings you fight for—Jacob (Gen. 32:24–26).**

* Blessings that follow you—the psalmist
  (Ps. 1:1–6).
* Blessings that fall on you—Peter
  (Acts 2:1–14).

It is time to leave your second day curse and to enter into your Third Day blessing. There will come a time where no one will be left standing. There will come a time as in Solomon's porch where everyone will be healed. That day is coming, friend. The day of the blessing is coming.

THE LAMB ON THE MULE AND THE LION ON THE HORSE

The next day a great multitude that had come to the feast, when they heard that Jesus was coming to Jerusalem, took branches of palm trees and went out to meet Him, and cried out: "Hosanna! Blessed is He who comes in the name of the LORD! The King of Israel!" Then Jesus, when He had found a young donkey, sat on it; as it is written: "Fear not, daughter of Zion; behold, your King is coming, sitting on a donkey's colt."
—JOHN 12:12–15

224

The Lamb

* The last time Jesus Christ entered Jerusalem, He was a Lamb on a donkey.
* The next time He enters Jerusalem, He will be a Lion riding on a horse.

Friend, you must come into the third day. You must ride on

the blessings that God has enabled you to have. You must ride on the circumstances and the situations that God has permitted you to go through. This is our triumphal entry. When the ark of the covenant returned to Jerusalem, David awaited it with celebration and joy. When Jesus Christ entered Jerusalem, it was the New Testament realization that the ark of the covenant was coming in. In the Old Testament, it was brought in by selected Levites. In the New Testament, Christ came in on a mule. Why did He enter?

You are blessed in the third day in order to break the curses of the second day!

Jesus entered to break sin in His house and to clean the temple:

> *Then Jesus went into the temple of God and drove out all those who bought and sold in the temple, and overturned the tables of the money changers and the seats of those who sold doves. And He said to them, "It is written, 'My house shall be called a house of prayer,' but you have made it a 'den of thieves.'"*—MATTHEW 21:12–13

Another instance of breaking took place during the last week of Jesus' life on earth. This time a woman broke an expensive alabaster jar and anointed the feet of Jesus with the costly perfume that poured out.

225

> *And behold, a woman in the city who was a sinner, when she knew that Jesus sat at the table in the Pharisee's house, brought an alabaster flask of fragrant oil, and stood at His feet behind Him weeping; and she*

*began to wash His feet with her tears, and
wiped them with the hair of her head; and
she kissed His feet and anointed them with
the fragrant oil.*—LUKE 7:37–38

On the night of Jesus' arrest, He broke bread with His
disciples and ate the last supper with them.

*And as they were eating, Jesus took bread,
blessed and broke it, and gave it to the
disciples and said, "Take, eat; this is My
body."*—MATTHEW 26:26

Christ entered to break. To break sin . . . to
break the alabaster jar . . . **and to break bread.**

We began this book by explaining that the Third Day worshiper is both a lamb and a lion. Here in this chapter we
come face to face with *the Lamb*—Jesus Christ, who takes
away the sin of the world (John 1:29). **What can wash
away my sin?** Not the blood of the lion . . . **not
the blood of the eagle . . . not the blood of the
bear . . . only the blood of *the Lamb* could—and
did—do it!**

The mule

We must understand that the mule was normally rejected
by people because it was weak. All the horses would mock
the mule and say, "You are just a mule. You will never
amount to anything." Oh yes, but the mule knew . . . one
day . . . one day . . .

I can imagine Jesus evaluating which animal He would
use to bring Him into Jerusalem:

❋ **"I do not want the black stallion;**
❋ **"I do not want the perfect one;**

226

✳ "I do not want the beautiful one;
✳ "I do not want the popular one."

I can hear Him saying, "I used those in the 1920s, '30s, '40s, '50s, '60s, '70s and '80s." In the third day, Jesus Christ selects the Third Day worshiper . . . the Third Day church . . . and the Third Day ministry.

✳ "On which Third Day worshipers will I write?
✳ "On which Third Day churches will I pour out My presence?
✳ "Which Third Day ministries will I set ablaze with My fire?"

He will not take the perfect one or the beautiful one or the popular one. He will declare, "Give me the mule. I like the weak. I like the hurting. I like the bruised. I will ride on them." This is your day, friend.

I can imagine that the mule on that day in Jerusalem was thinking, *I feel something*. He called to those other animals and said, "Hey guys, look at me now.

✳ "I never won the Kentucky Derby;
✳ "I never won the Belmont Stakes;
✳ "I never participated in the Jerusalem Run.

"But guess who is carrying the King of kings?!

✳ "I am carrying in the anointing,
✳ "I am carrying the cross;
✳ "I am carrying in the glory."

227

Hey, horse . . . hey, eagle . . . hey, bear . . . hey, denominational man . . . hey, Mr. Theologian . . . hey, Dr. Scholar . . . hey, Mrs. Religion . . . hey, Mr. Pharisee . . . guess who is carrying in the glory?

God will usher in His glory—not on a thoroughbred

horse . . . not through the most selective of ministries—He will usher in His glory on a mule. Jesus Christ is entering triumphantly upon the face of this planet one more time with His glory—and He will do so on mules.

> For too long we have worshiped the individual who carries the anointing rather than the One who gives the anointing.

I am a mule, but it's not about the donkey or the mule—the third day is all about the Lamb.

> ✳ **For too long we have been worshiping the donkey.**
> ✳ **The One we should be worshiping is the Lamb.**

For too long we have worshiped the men and women of God who have been used for God's honor and glory. Friend, don't worship the donkey—worship the Lamb.

You are reading this book by someone who recognizes that I am a mere donkey—but I know I carry a divine Lamb on top of me.

The palms

Knowing that fact helps me to understand the revelation of palms. When we carry the divine Lamb into our cities, into our communities, into our world, many will praise. Many will come to see and say, "Blessed is He who comes in the name of the LORD!" (Mark 11:9).

Friend, understand that in the third day, the tree branches were ripped off the trees. You must rip your praise off the tree. It is not good enough unless it is ripped.

I have been broken because I am about to give God the highest praise. You have been broken to praise. My praise will break the back of the devil. Understand that not only did they wave the palm branches—they also threw them on the floor.

✳ **You must walk on your praise.**
✳ **You must bathe your past with praise.**

People use palm branches to refresh themselves with a cool wind. Oh, hallelujah, one praise cools you off. But many branches make a shadow. Many praises create a shadow, and there you can hide in the third day. Cover yourself with the waving palms of praise above you and with the falling *When your heart is broken, it gives God the highest praise.* palms of praise below you. Cover yourself with praise. In the third day, Jesus Christ will rise triumphantly. Many will come to glorify His name.

✳ **Upon whom will He come into Jerusalem?**
✳ **Upon whom will He come into New York City?**
✳ **Upon whom will He come into North America?**
✳ **Upon whom will He come into South America?**
✳ **Upon whom will He come into Africa?**
✳ **Upon whom will He come into Europe?**
✳ **Upon whom will He come into Asia?**
✳ **Upon whom will He come into Australia?**
✳ **Upon whom will He ride?**
✳ **He will ride on the mule.**
✳ **He will ride on the donkey.**
✳ **He will ride on the rejected one.**
✳ **He will ride on the weak one.**
✳ **He will ride on the undesirable.**

229

As He sits astride these humble, willing Third Day worshipers, it is He who will receive all the honor, all the glory and all the praise.

Are you Third Day?

Living in His Sight: Third Day Kings

He is alive, *He is alive*, **He is alive.** Resounding news. Exclamation and utter joy catapulted to the heavenlies as the angels, the Father and Creation, in one orchestrated sound of perfect harmony, shouted, "He's alive!"

* As if they never knew
* As if there were ever a question
* As if someone doubted for a brief moment

No, no one doubted. It was the Father's plan. Creation anticipated it . . . the Father predestined it . . . the world knew it. Nevertheless, the accomplishment brought not hope for divinity, but faith for humanity.

* The greatest Third Day occurrence was not Abraham offering Isaac at the altar.

* The greatest Third Day occurrence was not Jonah being vomited from the whale.

* The greatest Third Day occurrence was not Jesus converting water into wine.

231

The greatest Third Day occurrence was the Resurrection of the Messiah!

*And He said to them, "Go, tell that fox,
'Behold, I cast out demons and perform
cures today and tomorrow, and the third
day I shall be perfected.'"*—LUKE 13:32

*They will scourge Him and kill Him. And
the third day He will rise again.*—LUKE 18:33

*Him God raised up on the third day, and
showed Him openly.*—ACTS 10:40

Jesus Christ, the Lamb of glory, resurrected from the dead.

* I want the devil to know.
* I want Muhammad to know.
* I want Buddha to know.
* I want Hitler to know.
* I want Lenin to know.
* I want Marx to know.
* I want Floyd to know.
* I want Darwin to know.
* I want witches to know.
* I want warlocks to know.
* I want New Agers to know.

I got up this morning and checked. The tomb is empty,
and the grave is wide open!

* The tomb is still empty.
* The grave is still open.
* Jesus Christ is still alive.

*Jesus said to her, "I am the resurrection
and the life. He who believes in Me, though
he may die, he shall live."*—JOHN 11:25

*The thief does not come except to steal, and
to kill, and to destroy. I have come that*

they may have life, and that they may have it more abundantly.—JOHN 10:10

Christ moved out of the grave so that He could move into our hearts.

SEPARATION, ORIGINATION, ACCUSATION AND DESTINATION

On the third day, four things were broken:

> ✳ **The veil was broken—representing the separation.**

> ✳ **The earth was broken—representing the origination.**

> ✳ **The rocks were broken—representing the accusation.**

> ✳ **The grave was broken—representing the destination.**

The grave: destination

> *And the graves were opened; and many bodies of the saints who had fallen asleep were raised.—MATTHEW 27:52*

In the grave—the destination of eternal death—we see dead men and women walking. You and I are Third Day 233 zombies. Why?

> ✳ **I am dead, yet I am alive.**
> ✳ **I am crucified, yet I am living.**

But let me tell you something wonderful, a mystery I'll probably never fully understand. We're not all going to die—but we are all going to be changed. You hear a blast to end all blasts from a

ARE YOU A THIRD DAY CHRISTIAN?

*trumpet, and in the time that you look up and blink your eyes—
it's over. On signal from that trumpet from heaven, the dead
will be up and out of their graves, beyond the reach of death,
never to die again. At the same moment and in the same way,
we'll all be changed. In the resurrection scheme of things, this has
to happen: everything perishable taken off the shelves and
replaced by the imperishable, this mortal replaced by the
immortal. Then the saying will come true: "Death swallowed
by triumphant Life! Who got the last word, oh, Death? Oh,
Death, who's afraid of you now?"*

—1 C{ORINTHIANS} 15:51–55, T{HE} M{ESSAGE}

In the third day, we will boldly speak to death and the
grave, saying . . .

✳ **"O death, where is thy sting?**
✳ **"O grave, where is thy victory?"**
—1 C{ORINTHIANS} 15:55, KJV

Death no longer has a hold on you. The grave no longer
has a hold on you. Not only is death annihilated . . . not
only is your destination reversed . . . but so also are the
rocks, which represent the accusation broken in two.

*Then, behold, the veil of the temple was
torn in two from top to bottom; and the
earth quaked, and the rocks were split.*
—M{ATTHEW} 27:51

234

The thing that was holding you back is broken; the stone
was split. It may be the same accusing stones that could
have been hurled at the adulteress woman (John 8:2–11).

Yes, friend, the stones that the Pharisees attempted to use
against the adulteress woman were broken in half in the
third day. **The stones accusing you have been**

broken. Those accusations will be broken before they hit you. **The allegations will be broken before they hit you. The things that were holding you back will be broken before they impede you.**

THE BLOOD OF JESUS

The earth, or the dust of humanity, dies. Divinity lives. The veil is separated. What was used to complete these things? The blood did it. A proud father likes to show off the child he adores. He thrills to see his daughter dressed in a new Easter dress and saying, "Papa, do you like my dress?" Proud parents show off their kids.

> In the third day the accusations will break before they hit you.

Jesus says to us, "Get up; show Daddy what My blood has done for you. Stand before the Father and say, 'Daddy, do you like my robe of righteousness?'" In the third day, we recognize the power of the blood. The only way in is by the blood.

> *. . . but with the precious blood of Christ, as of a lamb without blemish and without spot.*—1 PETER 1:19

> ✳ **You cannot praise yourself into the holy of holies.**
> ✳ **You cannot dance yourself into the holy of holies.**
> ✳ **You cannot tithe your way into the holy of holies.**

235

There is only one way in, and that is through the blood. I have news for you. You and I were not ever worthy of going in.

✳ But by the blood we can praise Him.
✳ By the blood we can worship Him.
✳ By the blood we can honor Him.
✳ By the blood we can glorify Him.
✳ By the blood we can exalt Him.
✳ By the blood we can magnify Him.

ARISE AS THIRD DAY KINGS

Jesus Christ was resurrected as a king. It is no wonder that when Mary initially encountered the risen Christ . . . when the disciples encountered the risen Christ . . . there was a bit of perplexity and confusion. Why? Because He was different. He no longer wore the cross of a martyr—Christ was wearing the robes of a king.

> *Now it happened on the third day that Esther put on her royal robes and stood in the inner court of the king's palace, across from the king's house, while the king sat on his royal throne in the royal house, facing the entrance of the house.*—ESTHER 5:1

In the third day, we put on our royal apparel. In the third day we no longer function as first day slaves or second day victims—we function as Third Day kings.

236

The devil's greatest lie has been to deceive the body of Christ into believing that we are slaves and victims. "But," you may ask, "isn't Jesus the only king?"

No, Jesus is not the only king. The Bible says that He is the King above all kings. He reigns. He is the King of kings, and He reigns over other kings.

You are either a first day slave, a second day victim or a Third Day king!

And they sang a new song, saying: "You are worthy to take the scroll, and to open its seals; for You were slain, and have redeemed us to God by Your blood out of every tribe and tongue and people and nation, and have made us kings and priests to our God; and we shall reign on the earth."—REVELATION 5:9–10

✳ **I do not see drug addicts in our churches.**
✳ **I do not see sinners in our churches.**
✳ **I do not see religious folks in our churches.**
✳ **I do not see victims in our churches.**
✳ **I do not see slaves in our churches.**

But I do see

✳ **apostles,**
✳ **prophets,**
✳ **pastors,**
✳ **evangelists,**
✳ **teachers.**

I see kings!

In the third day, we no longer have churches full of drug addicts, sinners, religious folks, victims or slaves. We have churches full of apostles, pastors, evangelists, prophets, teachers—I see kings.

237

All the kings of the earth shall praise You, O LORD, when they hear the words of Your mouth.—PSALM 138:4

When you praise you are a king.

How do you know that you are a king? By your praise. Let your praise be a royal praise. Let it be a kingly praise.

But the king will rejoice in God; everyone who swears by Him shall glory; but the mouth of those who speak lies shall be stopped.—PSALM 63:11

WHAT DO THIRD DAY KINGS DO?

✳ King David built a city for God.
✳ King Solomon built a temple for God.
✳ But Third Day kings build a kingdom for God.

In the third day we will no longer build individual churches **or individual ministries or individual empires. We will get together and build the kingdom of almighty God.**

But you are a chosen generation, a royal priesthood, a holy nation, His own special people, that you may proclaim the praises of Him who called you out of darkness into His marvelous light.—1 PETER 2:9

Third Day kings do four things: praise, rule, decree and pardon.

Praise

238 Praise, in essence, is a recognition of the deity and sovereignty of God. A king is one who is recognized in authority and power. Therefore, a king cannot truly exist until he recognizes that the authority and power he has received did not originate from himself, but from the God above him who is sovereign and divine. When he recognizes that, he can accept the fact of ever-existing power that can only be bestowed from someone supreme—that being the chief King. That is why our God is not just a Creator, but more importantly, He is the King of kings.

A Third Day king is a king of praise. Upon his heart, mouth and lips rests a living, moving and active recognition of the King over all kings. It is for that reason that the psalmist declared:

> *For God is the King of all the earth; sing to him a psalm of praise.*—PSALM 47:7, NIV

Rule

As the King of kings, Jesus rules over all things and people, including the kingdom of hell and Satan himself. Why is Satan the prince of darkness? Because he is not a king. Even with all his power and dominion, he recognized that his position is limited and not kingly.

Jesus is the King!

As the apostle Paul wrote to the church in Rome, divinely stating that Christ is the firstborn among many brethren, the irrevocable truth is that we are one with Him. As a result, you and I are kings, and He is the King of kings— us. You, my brother and sister, are a king and a queen. Therefore, because all authority was given to Christ, and through Him we operate in His divine nature, you and I as kings and queens rule with power and dominion.

You have the power to rule over things in your life!

* No matter the situation
* No matter the circumstance
* No matter the condition

239

In the name of Jesus, in the third day you rule over things. And as you rule, you do three things:

* You go to the tomb.
* You roll back the stone.
* You sit on that stone.

There was a violent earthquake, for an angel of the Lord came down from heaven and, going to the tomb, rolled back the stone and sat on it.—Matthew 28:2, NIV

✳ **If an angel who has not been washed with the blood of Christ . . .**
✳ **If an angel who has not been sealed with the Holy Spirit . . .**
✳ **If an angel who has not been filled with the Father's glory . . .**

. . . could go to the tomb, roll back the stone and sit on it, then how much more can you and I do even greater as kings that are governed by Christ?

Friend, you have the kingly authority to rule over the things that surround you, because there is One named Jesus who rules over the things that are within you!

As long as Christ the King rules within you, you—His king—will rule those things around you. Even the earth and everything in it are subject to you because the King of kings rules over you.

The earth is the Lord*'s, and everything in it, the world, and all who live in it; for he founded it upon the seas and established it upon the waters. Who may ascend the hill of the* Lord*? Who may stand in his holy place? He who has clean hands and a pure heart, who does not lift up his soul to an idol or swear by what is false. He will receive blessing from the* Lord *and vindication from God his Savior. Such is the generation of those who seek him, who* *seek your face, O God of Jacob. Lift up your heads, O you gates; be lifted up, you ancient doors, that the King of glory may come in. Who is this King of glory? The LORD strong and mighty, the LORD mighty in battle. Lift up your heads, O you gates; lift them up, you ancient doors, that the King of glory may come in. Who is he, this King of glory? The LORD Almighty— he is the King of glory.—PSALM 24, NIV*

Prior to the fall of man, God ruled over Adam and ordered Adam to rule over creation. Therefore, in the third day of revival, raising up and living in His sight, you must rule. Go to the tomb of the areas of your life that are buried, roll back the stones that are impeding His glory from entering in and finally, do not just get rid of that stone—sit on it!

Make your situation, circumstance and condition a throne that you rule upon, rule from and rule over!

It is time to rule in Jesus' name. He is the King of kings. And in Him, through Him and by Him, we are kings and queens!

Decree

But when Herod's birthday was celebrated, the daughter of Herodias danced before them and pleased Herod. Therefore he promised with an oath to give her whatever she might ask. So she, having been prompted by her mother, said, "Give me John the Baptist's head here on a platter."—MATTHEW 14:6–8

If King Herod had the power to put John's head on a platter at the request of a girl who danced before him, what power can King Jesus exert at our request if we dance before Him? Whose head will He put on a platter? We have the power to dance before the Lord, and we can ask King Jesus to give us the head of the enemy on a platter. When you dance before the King of kings, He will put the enemy's head on a platter.

It is time for you to dance before the King. When you dance before the King, He will put the head of the enemy on a platter. That is the decree of a king. We need kings in our churches. We need kings at our altars.

The church that I pastor is a church of kings and queens. They may not look like kings to those around them . . .

* **They may look like former drug addicts and prostitutes.**
* **They may look like former homosexuals and alienated individuals.**
* **They may look like present-day Wall Street brokers and bankers.**
* **They may look like merchants and police officers.**

But in reality they are Third Day kings.

In the second day, they had a humanistic label. But in the third day, they realize that they have been chosen to be kings.

> *But you are a chosen generation, a royal priesthood, a holy nation, His own special people, that you may proclaim the praises of Him who called you out of darkness into His marvelous light.*—1 PETER 2:9

✳ I pastor Third Day kings.
✳ I fellowship with Third Day kings.
✳ I pray with Third Day kings.
✳ I praise with Third Day kings.
✳ I worship with Third Day kings.
✳ I fast with Third Day kings.

Dance, king, dance! As you dance, every step, every move and every motion will be a living, vibrant and active decree that will place the head of your enemy on a platter. So dance! But this is not just any dance.

✳ More than a physical expression . . .
✳ more than an emotional thrill . . .
✳ more than a psychological understanding . . .

We live with the anointing of kings to praise . . . to rule . . . to decree . . . and to pardon.

. . . this dance is the continuous move of your soul dancing with God's Spirit to a resurrection rhythm, where the orchestra of grace is playing the song of your redemption. This song and dance is revived, raised up and living in the sight of your God. And now that you are dancing, tell the King of kings to place the head of your enemy on the platter.

243

✳ Put depression on the platter.
✳ Put oppression on the platter.
✳ Put sickness on the platter.
✳ Put bondage on the platter.
✳ Put poverty on the platter.
✳ Put death on the platter.
✳ Put it all on the platter!

Power to pardon

Third Day kings have the power to forgive debts.

Forgive us our debts, as we forgive our debtors.—MATTHEW 6:12

The most powerful ability that a Third Day king has is to pardon a wrongdoer. When you learn to forgive, then legitimately you are a Third Day king.

* Until you learn to forgive those who have done you wrong,
* until you learn to forgive those who have failed you,
* until you learn to forgive those who have fallen short of your expectations,

. . . you will never be a Third Day king.

GLORIFIED, BUT NOT RECOGNIZED

On the third day Jesus Christ was resurrected as a king. It is important to note that when He was glorified He was not immediately recognized. In the third day they are not going to recognize us.

* They might not give you recognition, but they are going to touch you.
* They might not give you recognition, but they are going to feel your wounds.
* They might not give you recognition, but they will follow you.
* They might not give you recognition, but they will see you ascend.

In our case, when our King of kings returns to take us back to His kingdom to rule and reign, those on earth may see us disappear right before their eyes.

WHOM WILL HE MAKE KINGS?

In the third day whom does God make kings? He calls fisherman . . . working men . . . those who have denied Him . . . to Himself and makes them kings.

When you have lost it all, God will make you a king.

> *Therefore that disciple whom Jesus loved said to Peter, "It is the Lord!" Now when Simon Peter heard that it was the Lord, he put on his outer garment (for he had removed it), and plunged into the sea.*
>
> —JOHN 21:7

He will prepare a meal for you. He will call you out to fish, to feed and to follow. Get ready. It is your time to be a Third Day king. We are a royal priesthood, and we are kings. We can go into the holy of holies. We have the bells, and the bells are ringing in the holy of holies.

I would rather die in His presence than live outside of His presence.

In the third day, we no longer have a rope tied around our waist. We have cut off the rope. That second day religious rope has been cut off, because even if we die, we will die in His presence.

If we die in His presence, we are alive in His glory. I would rather die in the presence of God than to live in the presence of men.

245

❋ Gather the body together.
❋ Gather the saints together.
❋ Gather the believers together.
❋ Gather the worshipers together.

You are either a first day slave, a second day victim or a Third Day king. Therefore, the question stands before you:

Are you Third Day?

* ✳ **Are you a second day lamb or a Third Day lion?**
* ✳ **Are you a second day worker or a Third Day worshiper?**
* ✳ **Are you a second day grape or Third Day wine?**
* ✳ **Are you a second day mountain mover or a Third Day mountain climber?**
* ✳ **Are you a second day follower or a Third Day freak?**
* ✳ **Are you a second day victim or a Third Day king?**

You are Third Day— Welcome to the Third Day

THE FINAL CLASH

All the nations are gathered together against the children of God. The nations have gathered in the valley of Megiddo.

* ✳ **They are ready to annihilate.**
* ✳ **They are ready to destroy.**
* ✳ **They are ready to nullify.**

246 The earth is prepared. Seven years have passed. Now it is time!

* ✳ **Jesus Christ mounts the horse.**
* ✳ **He has a sword in His hands.**
* ✳ **There is fire burning in His eyes.**
* ✳ **He wears a cross that covers one side of His chest down to His waist.**

He gets the armies of God together as they stand at

attention. And in one resounding voice He utters . . .

"Are you ready?"

Immediately the archangels approach him and say, "We shall ride with You, and we shall fight!"

Jesus Christ replies, "I know you will, but there is another army.

> ✳ **"There is an army that will accompany Me in this battle.**
> ✳ **"They will spearhead this battle with Me."**

Who can the army be?

At that moment, Christ calls upon the army.

> ✳ **The body**
> ✳ **The church**
> ✳ **The bride**

The Third Day worshipers

He calls them all out. Those who have been redeemed by the blood of the Lamb take their positions.

He calls out,

> ✳ **"Who will fight with Me?**
> ✳ **"Who will ride with Me?"**

On that day, you will understand the true value of being third day, for we shall ride with Him, and we shall rule with Him.

YOU ARE THIRD DAY!

247

CALVARY WORSHIP CENTER TO
Third Day Worship Center

On September 13, 1998, birth was given to Calvary Worship Center. Senior pastors Samuel and Eva Rodriguez founded this ministry as a multicultural church consisting of three congregations—English, Spanish and Portuguese speaking.

✳ **The growth of approximately 90 worshipers to 1,500 worshipers in less than two years was recognized internationally.**

✳ **The television and radio programs reaching 108 and 48 countries respectively were recognized as one of the most listened to programs of each hosting station.**

✳ **Calvary Worship Center churches were planted in the United States and South America.**

✳ **Reverend Rodriguez traveled throughout the United States, the Caribbean and Central and South America ministering the Word of God to English- and Spanish-speaking believers.**

This ministry was considered to be very successful. However, it was a first and second day church. But in the third month of its existence, a divine occurrence happened within the lives of senior pastors Samuel and Eva Rodriguez. God spoke beyond their body, mind and soul and into their spirit as He declared and demonstrated the message of the Third Day.

After two days He will revive us; on the third day He will raise us up, that we may live in His sight.—HOSEA 6:2

From that time, God began a revolution at Calvary Worship Center as the sermons, teachings, praise, worship and intercession escalated from the first and second day into the Third Day. No longer would this church focus on building its own name, identity and kingdom, but would rather build, plant and advance the kingdom of God.

Consequently, Calvary Worship Center was born, crucified and buried. On June 18, 2000, the THIRD DAY WORSHIP CENTER was born! The mission:

To engage, empower, enrich and enhance
individuals, families, neighborhoods and
communities for the service of Jesus Christ with
the resurrection power for revival, raising up
and living in His sight, throughout the world.

Therefore, we invite you to visit us whenever you are in the area or on the Internet.

THIRD DAY WORSHIP CENTER
2252 Forest Avenue • Staten Island, NY 10303
(718) 273-1111
www.thirddayworshipcenter.org